THE REVD RICHARD SUTCLIFFE is a part-time priest in the Church of England, living in a small village in Hampshire. After leaving university and qualifying as an accountant, he worked for most of his career in London as a policy maker in Financial Regulation. After the pandemic, he decided to take early retirement from his life in London and to enjoy a quieter life in the countryside, with his family and his dogs.

Richard wrote *Finding Mac* as a way to record and share stories with his family and friends, and to help the memories of Mac to live on. He has published an article in the *Church Times* about being a bereaved father and also took part in a conversation for the Radio 4 programme The Listening Project.

He now works part-time in his local churches as part of a wider ministry team. This gives him plenty of time to spend with his sister, his nephews and their growing families, and to indulge in his interest in collecting art.

Finding Mac
A journey of adoption, love and loss

The Reverend
RICHARD SUTCLIFFE

SilverWood

Published in 2024 by SilverWood Books

SilverWood Books Ltd
14 Small Street, Bristol, BS1 1DE, United Kingdom
www.silverwoodbooks.co.uk

Text copyright © Richard Sutcliffe 2024
Images from the author's family collection

The right of Richard Sutcliffe to be identified as the author of this work has been asserted in accordance with the Copyright, Designs and Patents Act 1988 Sections 77 and 78.

All rights reserved. No part of this publication may be reproduced, stored in a retrieval system, or transmitted in any form or by any means, electronic, mechanical, photocopying, recording or otherwise, without prior permission of the copyright holder.

This book is based on the author's experiences. This work depicts actual events in the life of the author as truthfully as recollection permits. Some dialogue has been retold in a way that accurately evokes the meaning and feeling of what was said. The story, the experiences, and the words are the author's alone.

ISBN 978-1-80042-289-6 (paperback)
ISBN 978-1-80042-290-2 (hardback)
Also available as an ebook

British Library Cataloguing in Publication Data
A CIP catalogue record for this book is
available from the British Library

Page design and typesetting by SilverWood Books

Dedication

This book is dedicated to my family and friends and all of those people who have been there for me over the past few years.

But most of all it is for my soulmate, Swee, and our beautiful son, Mac. We were the perfect family and the memories live on. Our time together may have been short, but it shone like the brightest star. Love is all.

FINDING MAC

Contents

Foreword	Why Did I Write This Book?	11
Chapter 1	Introductions	15
Chapter 2	Back to the Beginning	26
Chapter 3	14 November 2008	39
Chapter 4	The First Week	49
Chapter 5	The Honeymoon Period (and Beyond!)	58
Chapter 6	Primary School	72
Chapter 7	Contact	85
Chapter 8	Special Occasions	96
Chapter 9	First Holidays	106
Chapter 10	Mac and Church	118
Chapter 11	Secondary School	129
Chapter 12	Growing Up	138
Chapter 13	New School, New Start	150
Chapter 14	Pets, Friends, Girlfriends and Growing Older	160
Chapter 15	US Holidays (Florida)	171
Chapter 16	US Holidays (New York and North Carolina)	182
Chapter 17	Uganda and Turning Sixteen	192
Chapter 18	14 October 2016	200
Chapter 19	The Next Few Weeks	208
Chapter 20	5 November 2016	219
Chapter 21	The First Year	227
Chapter 22	Being Mac's Mum: Thoughts from Swee	242
Chapter 23	Life After Mac	248
Chapter 24	Final Thoughts	255

Foreword

Why Did I Write This Book?

Modern families come together in all sorts of ways – one parent, two parents; same sex, opposite sex; planned, unplanned; biological, adopted. We have examples of different sorts of families all around us, and these examples inevitably inform our ideas of what our own families will be like – the way we want to be as parents; the number of children we think is ideal.

This book tells the story of how our little family came together, and the ups and downs as we got to know and love each other and become a successful family unit. Inevitably it focuses on the experience of adoption, and particularly the experience of adopting an older child. We adopted Mac when he was eight. Not uncommonly for a child adopted at that age, he had passed through a number of homes in his short life.

So I hope this account might help those who are considering undertaking the same journey that we took, or are already on that journey. This is not a manual of how one should go about bringing up an adopted child – I wouldn't presume to be able to tell anyone that! This is just a record of how one small family in rural

Hampshire made it work and got through the everyday challenges and excitements of becoming a new family.

Of course, much of what is here relates specifically to adoption and how it works in the United Kingdom, but I hope that there is something here for all sorts of families as they enjoy and struggle to help their healthy, gorgeous, funny, moody and intelligent children as they grow into wonderful adults. I know that for me the greatest achievement of my life has been to see Mac grow into a kind, loving, thoughtful and hilarious young man.

I also wanted to record all of these memories somewhere. As I have grown older, and close family members have died, I've realised that many of the stories that go with the photos we keep are lost. I used to love sitting with my grandma, listening to her stories of living through two world wars. I used to love asking her questions, especially if I had forgotten some important part of the narrative. But now I cannot ask her, and I regret that there is no permanent record anywhere of all of those stories.

When we first adopted Mac, we put together albums of pictures and memories called 'Life Story Books' – these are great ways to help an adopted child to understand where they have come from and how they fit into their new family. My wife, Swee, was artistic and created beautiful books, and continued to put them together each year for Mac so that he could look back on everything and enjoy the new memories we were making as a family. I hope that my account here will add to those wonderful books that Swee created.

I used to contemplate, when we were thinking about and going through the adoption process, the fact that our child must already be born, and wonder what they were doing and how they were. It is hard to think too much about their past – it being something that you were not part of – and yet you love your child and your natural parental instincts can make you wish that you could have been there sooner to save them from all the hurt.

The stories here tell of how Swee and I found our son, Mac. Through recounting the events of his growing up, this book describes how we continued to peel away the layers, to help to fill in the missing pieces from his early life – in short, how we continued to find Mac. And eventually it tells how Mac grew up and found the person inside that he was happy with – how he found Mac himself.

As an adoptive parent, I sometimes felt that we had 'borrowed' Mac. As he was not our biological son, it felt that we might only have him for a short time. There was always the slight risk that, when he was old enough, he might choose to go back to his biological family and leave us behind. But in some ways, as parents, our children are always borrowed. We are successful when we let them go to pursue their own lives and build their own families. We can make memories together; we can teach them unconditional love and hope that they will value it and love us in return. The memories we make are important: they can outlive us all. As I grow older, I realise that life is short, and I don't want the memories that my family made to die with us when I finally shuffle off this mortal coil.

Finally, I hope that what you see in this account are stories based on love. The pure, unconditional love between a parent and a child is the most precious thing and I am so glad to have been lucky to experience it. Love is the most important thing.

> *Love is patient, love is kind. It does not envy, it does not boast, it is not proud. It does not dishonour others, it is not self-seeking, it is not easily angered, it keeps no record of*

wrongs. Love does not delight in evil but rejoices with the truth. It always protects, always trusts, always hopes, always perseveres...

And now these three remain: faith, hope and love. But the greatest of these is love.

(Extract from St Paul's first letter to the Corinthians, chapter 13)

Chapter 1

Introductions

First meeting

It was a sultry summer afternoon in a small village in Hampshire. Two people were sitting on the bench outside the village shop. To any passer-by it would have looked like a normal day – nothing seemed out of the ordinary; just a couple enjoying a quiet, lazy, sunny afternoon in a beautiful picture-postcard village. But if you looked closely, you might have noticed that the couple perhaps looked anxious, and that they weren't talking. You might have noticed that they looked a little too closely at each car that drove past them. You might have noticed that they looked slightly emotional. You might have noticed that the same two people kept popping out of the shop to ask a question and look around expectantly.

But today – a normal day in August 2008 – was about to become the most significant moment in the couple's lives. That couple was my wife, Swee, and me, and today was going to be the day that we met Mac.

A VW Polo pulled up. Out came our social worker, Denise, followed by a small, wan, skinny eight-year-old. He was dressed in his school uniform of red jumper and charcoal trousers, all covered with a thin, slightly worn cagoule. He and Denise went to the boot of the car and took out his scooter.

"Do you want to see my skills?" he said.

"Of course," I replied.

And with that, he scooted onto the recreation ground and started to try to do some tricks – trying hard to impress, as if he was in some juvenile talent contest; doing everything to impress us and win the competition. There was an intensity and a concentration in his trying to show how good he was with his scooter that was at once endearing and heartbreaking. Here was a little boy, desperate for his own new family, trying to make sure that finally he would be the one to be chosen.

Of course, what Mac didn't know was that we were already in love – as soon as we saw his face, we knew he was ours, we knew he was our son and that our family was complete. As soon as we saw him, we were desperate to get him home and love him and spoil him and give him all the things that we had dreamed about. However, we all needed to play things cool. This meeting was unorthodox. The usual wisdom in the adoption process is that there should be no meetings between prospective parents and child until after there has been a formal matching decision – that is, a panel of the great and the good working for the adoption agency have decided that they agree that the match is a good one and should go ahead.

But this situation was slightly different. Although our social workers and their management had agreed that this was a good potential pairing, the formal process had not yet been initiated. This was because Mac had expressed a desire to have some say in the process himself. He had already had a failed adoptive placement, which had been successful for his younger brother. (Mac also had two older brothers who had gone to live with other members of the family.) In fact, at eight years old he was now at an age where the received wisdom is that adoption is less likely to be successful and permanent fostering is a more likely option. But Mac's determination to have a family of his own – to be like his younger brother – won through, and the social workers were prepared to let him have some say in the selection. So, rather than him trying to impress us, Swee and I were trying hard to make sure that he would want to be with us and that he would be happy with the match.

After he had scooted around a little more, we went into the local shop to get him a snack. He chose his favourite: a thick chocolate milkshake and some extra-strong mints. My mum was one of the volunteers in the shop, and was working there that afternoon. However, all of the family had been given strict instructions not to identify themselves at that point as it was important not to overwhelm Mac with too much information. She took his money and pretended that she didn't know that anything special was going on. Then my dad arrived, quickly followed by my sister – all by coincidence, of course! Actually, many of our friends happened to pop over to the shop and the recreation ground that afternoon. One of the notable things about living in a village is that news travels fast with no effort at all, especially when you are trying to keep a secret.

After a little more playing in the playground, it was time for Mac to go home. He packed up his scooter and got into the back of the car, and Denise drove him back to his foster home in the New Forest.

We sat down and Mum joined us, and we just sobbed for joy; the years of stress and uncertainty finally coming out in our tears. It was so unreal.

"He's so beautiful!" Swee said.

I wasn't able to speak – I didn't know that I could add anything of any use to the conversation. The meeting had been profound and one of the most emotional of our lives as everything we had read about Mac became real. Love was instant. There was a hormonal surge urging us to care for this quirky, loving, sad, damaged and charming boy. We had found Mac, and it was as if some primeval urge had kicked in and was compelling us to look after and protect this small, vulnerable child. There was a need to give him all of the things that he had never had, and to right all of the wrongs that had been done to him in his life so far.

Denise called later that night to say how well she thought the meeting had gone, and that it had had a profound effect on Mac as well. As she was driving him home, he'd opened up to her in a way that he never had before, asking questions about his birth family and why things had happened the way they had, and why he had had to leave them. It seemed he was already emotionally preparing himself to join a new family – our family.

Sue and Mark

Now that the meeting had gone well, all was on for our panel to take place to approve the match so that Mac could move in. While we were waiting for that date, we were sent to meet his current foster carers, Sue and Mark. It wasn't billed as an approval meeting, but it was clear to us that if they didn't think we were up to the job, approval might well not be forthcoming.

So, one afternoon, Mac was sent away to play and we went to visit his foster home and foster parents. We followed our satnav as it took us to smaller and smaller roads through the New Forest. Finally, we came to a small group of houses in the middle of nowhere – the final one of these was Sue and Mark's.

I don't know about you, but I have always thought that certain buildings exude feelings. When you go into a cathedral or an old church, it's as if you can sense the years of prayer and stillness that have gone on there, giving the place an aura of holiness. It's as if the walls have absorbed the feelings. Well, there was something about Sue and Mark's house. It was modest and tidy, but it felt safe: there was a palpable feeling of the years of love, protection and healing that had gone on in that house as many foster children had passed through their hands.

We immediately liked Sue and Mark. It was the beginning of a friendship that we value to this day. We had great conversations about Mac, and for the first time we felt we were getting useful information about the boy who was to join our lives and what he was really like, rather than the sterile reports written by social workers. To anyone finding yourself in this situation: make the most of it. Prepare a list of the questions you want to ask and get as much information as you can. A child's foster carers, and especially very experienced carers like Sue and Mark, will be of huge value in ensuring that the placement will be successful. Don't be afraid to ask anything. Remember that they already love that child and want to make sure that their work is continued into a successful adoption.

Sue and Mark were used for some of the more difficult cases: those children who needed some extra care. Mac had been sent to them when his first adoptive placement broke down. He had been placed with another family with his younger brother with a view to adoption. However, while the placement had worked for his brother, it was not successful for Mac, and the unusual decision was taken to remove Mac and leave his brother, who went on to be adopted into that family. So, when Mac was taken to Sue and Mark's you can imagine that he was a very unhappy little boy. It is not exaggerating to say that without Sue and Mark's love and care (and a little help from their family and their beautiful Golden Retriever), Mac would never have been prepared to join a new family. We will always be grateful to them.

There is one thing that Mark said that remained with me, and it is a piece of wisdom that I share with anyone going through the process of adoption. As he walked us to our car, he said, "Macaully won't be the same little boy for you. He will change." At the time I didn't really know what he meant. But over time I began to understand. Mac did not let his full personality out with Sue and Mark. He understood that his home with them wasn't permanent and that he was marking time. It wasn't until he was in a home of his own and began to feel that it might become more permanent that his real personality started to show – the good bits and the naughty bits. Mark was right: when Mac moved in with us, we began the process of finding the real Mac. We eventually had a very different Mac to the one who had lived with Sue and Mark for a year.

Further meetings

Following these two meetings, we were sent to the approval panel. This group of people, made up of social workers, experienced adoptive parents, adoptees, and medical advisers, looked at our case to formally make the decision that we should be matched with Mac and that he should move in with us with a view to an adoption order being made as soon as it looked as if we were settling down as a new family. Panels are always nerve-racking. But the meeting went well, and we finally knew for sure that Mac would be moving in with us and we would begin our journey together.

The next stage was to make introductions and ease us into our relationship with Mac as we started to get to know him. After years of waiting, this stage of the adoption process starts to move very fast. The idea is for the child and the new parents to get to know each other before they move in permanently to their new home. It is a vital part of the attachment process. Sue and Mark had done this countless times and knew just how to make things work to their best.

So, first of all we went round to their house for tea. We went along ready to play and with a present in hand. Mac was always a very tactile boy, and it is interesting that he interacted very differently with me and Swee. With Swee, he just wanted to hug her – to sink into her chest like a baby and be enveloped by her. He hugged me as well, but was more interested in 'rough-and-tumble' games. He loved it if I turned him upside down, making him squeal with laughter.

We took Mac a small remote-controlled Dalek as a present. Sue and Mark's son shared his passion for *Doctor Who* with Mac – luckily, we liked the programme as well! We played for hours with that toy and I still have it to this day – somehow, it managed to survive the years.

We had a few other meetings with Mac at his foster home. Sometimes they were for special occasions, like the Halloween party for which we all dressed up as witches and wizards, went apple bobbing, and ate Halloween-themed food. But more important were the meetings during which we just did normal things: taking him for a bike ride, reading with him, or helping him with his homework. Sue and Mark knew that we needed to do the mundane things with Mac just as much as the exciting ones. These visits were short initially, giving us a chance to get used to each other. Sue and Mark would quietly disappear, but we all knew that they were nearby if we needed them at all. And there is no way of preparing for all of this; no training that helps. We always tried to just be as calm and friendly as possible, and to follow Mac's lead, hoping that he would grow to love us and accept us as his new parents. Of course, what we found out years later, when we talked about these times with an older Mac, was that he was desperately trying to make sure that we would love him; desperate not to be rejected again.

He also came to the village a few more times. First of all, he came with Denise again. By this time, we had sent Mac a book setting out all the details of the village and his new home: pictures of our family, our pets, the house, and his bedroom. These books are vitally important to adopted children. Their carers will go through them many times to get them ready for their move. The picture of Mac's bedroom made it clear that it was ready for him, but that he would be able to help us to redecorate so that it could be just as he wanted it.

However, when Mac came to visit with Denise it was decided that he shouldn't visit the house at this point as it was important not to overwhelm him. But he did want to meet our dogs, Rigby and Peller (named after the bra maker to the Queen!). Rigby and Peller were two Cavalier King Charles Spaniels that we'd received as a wedding present in 1999. They were now middle-aged boys, but truly loved anyone they met. Mac loved them immediately. He was used to dogs. Sue and Mark had a Golden Retriever, and Sue told us that their foster children could always be found cuddling him when things were particularly tough, quietly whispering all of their worries and sadnesses – an extra unpaid social worker.

So, we all met on the recreation ground again and took the dogs for a walk. Unfortunately, the afternoon turned into one of those late September storms when the heavens open for hours. Our social worker was adamant that we could not go to the house, so we ended up walking in the rain. I lent Mac my coat as his cagoule was not up to the job – this meant that by the end of our outing I was thoroughly soaked through to my pants.

Of course, Mac made the ban on visiting the house completely unnecessary as he knew exactly where it was when we walked past it. As we walked through the village he started to make his first requests: "When I move in, can I have a pet rat?" I was keen not to commit but, falling very quickly into 'dad mode', said we would think about it. (When Mac and I talked about this years later, he admitted that he had meant to ask for a hamster!)

At the end of the walk, we went to the local pub, The George, and played pool and ate chips. With Denise supervising Mac, Swee and I took the chance to pop back home, change into dry clothes, and bring a warm sweatshirt for Mac to change into. Sue later told me that he slept with that sweatshirt every night.

(It's funny how certain places play important parts in our lives. The George had brought my family to the village in 1979 when my parents bought and ran it. I was brought up there, and Swee used to work there at weekends with my sister. And now it was an important part of Mac's first visit to his new home – so much so that when Mac had the chance to add some middle names as part of the adoption process, one of them was George.)

More meetings followed, including overnight stays at our house. In my memories of these times there are a couple of things that stand out for me.

First is that you learn quickly from your mistakes. On a trip to Marwell Zoo we took Mac into the gift shop and were keen that he got a gift to remember this special day. However, we made it too difficult for him by saying to choose anything. We gave him no parameters and he just had no idea what to do – so he became upset and overwhelmed. My wife was always the sensible one, and quickly realised. She narrowed down the choice for him, and he chose a soft giraffe cushion that he loved to fall asleep with in the car. For a child who had had so little for so long, it was just too much to suddenly offer him anything he wanted.

Secondly, whenever we went to visit him at Sue and Mark's, Mac would always be looking out for us. His bedroom had a small window that looked out onto the road, and his little face would always be looking out expectantly, hoping that we would come as we'd said we would, and probably expecting each time that we might let him down. Children like Mac take a long time to trust that you will do what you say. His overriding experience of adults was that they promised things that didn't come true – we had to continue to be consistent to prove that we were different and would not let him down. I'll never forget the image of that face at the window.

The thing to remember about these meetings is that they are the start of making memories. For me, the making of shared memories is the most important thing – good, shared memories are so important as part of the bonding process, and to remember when times are tough. You want to be able to have those "Do you remember when…?" conversations with your kids.

One of my favourite memories from that time took place, again, at Marwell Zoo. This is a wonderful zoo close to where I live in Hampshire and had been a favourite place to visit when I was young, and I hoped that Mac would grow to love it as well. As we were about to leave, we saw an old man with a fantastic white beard. I pointed him out to Mac and said, "Look! There's Father Christmas in disguise – he's come to see if the boys and girls are being good!" Mac was completely taken in (and I have to say, the man did look remarkably like Father Christmas in casual clothes!). And this became a shared memory; one that we would often mention over the years.

All of these introductions and meetings happened over such a short number of weeks: from the last few weeks of August 2008, just after Mac's eighth birthday, to the middle of November. In those few weeks we started the journey to becoming a family. Looking back on this, and describing it above, I'm amazed at how much we were able to achieve in a relatively short time, bearing in mind that I was still working full-time, as my adoption leave wouldn't properly start until Mac moved in with us (my choice, as I wanted to spend as much time with him in our home as possible before I had to go back to work). But it was a strange, liminal time: on the edge of something life-changing, but just not quite there yet, and with the constant stress of social workers looking over your shoulder.

So eventually, with meetings and introductions all done, the day drew close for Mac to finally move in.

Chapter 2

Back to the Beginning

But before we come to moving-in day, I'd like to go back to the beginning to explain something of the journey that Swee and I went on before we first met Mac.

Growing up in an idyllic Hampshire village in the '80s, it was easy to think that life would work out in the way you planned. You would go to school, pass your exams, go to university, get a degree, get a 'good' job (whatever that was), get married, buy a house, get a dog and have children. I don't apologise for this overly simplistic view of the world. When I was growing up it was the example that I saw around me, and I knew that it was what I wanted for myself. And to be fair, my life did pretty much follow that path.

Looking back now, I loved growing up in the '70s and '80s. My childhood was safe, comfortable and carefree (in complete contrast to the childhood that Mac had experienced in his first eight years). I remember long summer holidays with warm, balmy evenings stretching out in front of us. Camping with friends in the garden, taking the opportunity to indulge in some illicit alcohol or tobacco. I remember clear, cold Bonfire Nights, with huge village bonfires, spectacular fireworks, jacket potatoes burning your hands, and cheap hot dogs with onions and tomato sauce. I remember twinkling candles in church at Christmastime, singing all our favourite carols, and looking forward to presents and playing games with the family. I remember cold, snowy winters, playing snowballs, building snowmen and sledging down hills. I remember acting in village plays, and particularly enjoying taking part in the village pantomimes. Even my teenage years were fairly painless. I was lucky enough to enjoy school, so homework wasn't a chore. Exams were a challenge I enjoyed.

There was a small hiccup at university. I was lucky enough to gain a place at Balliol College, Oxford, to study chemistry. Suddenly I no longer had the comfort of being at home, and I was surrounded by so many people who were so much more intelligent than me. I lost all confidence and eventually failed my degree. That was not how the plan was supposed to go. But I did enjoy university: I met some amazing people, and Oxford was a wonderful city to live in for four years. I also spent some time acting, including for a summer at the Edinburgh Fringe. My highlight was playing Bottom in an outdoor production of *A Midsummer Night's Dream* in the garden of The Queen's College. For that I got my best ever review, which read, 'Richard Sutcliffe's Bottom was a rotund tour de force.' The hiccup of my failed degree was soon overcome with a new job and qualifying as an accountant. My career moved on successfully and I enjoyed what I did.

After renting a few different places around South-West London, in 1998 I finally bought a lovely two-bedroomed terraced house in South Wimbledon: 80 Hardy Road. It was a lovely house; all polished floorboards, fireplaces, and a wonderful long garden. I needed help with the decorating, so my sister, Sandra, and her oldest and best friend, Swee, came to help me. I had known Swee for most of my life, so we always had fun when we all got together. She was also very artistic, and full of creative ideas for decorating the house.

Swee was able to spend more time on the house as Sandra needed to get back to her husband and sons, so inevitably Swee and I spent more time together. As we were both single, we started meeting up a few times, going to restaurants, and we spent hours on the phone, laughing at Saturday-night television talent programmes. We always shared the same sense of humour. Looking back now, it's easy to say that we were – and here's a wonderfully old-fashioned word – courting. But neither of us ever put a label on this.

Then on Valentine's Day 1999, a card dropped through my door. Although it was not signed and she had got someone else to write it, I knew instantly that it was from Swee. This threw me into all sorts of quandaries. What if we started something and it didn't work out? Was it better just to stay friends? What would Sandra say? After talking to my friends, I was no clearer about what to do. I felt that if things did not work out, it would be so awkward as Swee would always be part of the family as she was such a big part of Sandra's life. Was it really worth the risk?

My next move was probably somewhat unconventional. I invited Swee round for Saturday lunch. This must have been around May or June – certainly it was warm enough to sit outside. I cooked steak and crushed new potatoes. There was a certain awkwardness in the air – mostly because I was acting very strangely, I think. Then, after lunch, we came inside and I went upstairs and brought down the huge bunch of flowers that I had popped out that morning to get. And, sitting in the living room of 80 Hardy Road, I asked Swee to marry me. Clearly, this was not something that she had expected. And then I made another unexpected move. Having dropped the bombshell, I said, "Well, this is probably all a bit of a surprise, so I suggest you need to go home and think about it." And with that, I ushered her out of the house to her car and she made her way home. I went back in, and sat quietly.

Meanwhile, Swee had gone to her car and immediately phoned her sister, Annie. (I had made it clear that we couldn't talk to Sandra about my proposal.) According to Swee, the conversation went something like this:

Swee: Richard's just asked me to marry him!
Annie: What?!
Swee: I know!
Annie: What are you going to say?
Swee: Yes, of course.
Annie: You can't do that straight away – it's not cool!

So, thanks to my sister-in-law, Swee kept me waiting until Monday morning to give me her answer. Later that week, we met up in Hatton Garden, chose a ring (platinum with a half-carat diamond), and picked it up a few days later.

We were married on 11 December 1999, exactly a week after my parents celebrated their sapphire wedding anniversary (forty-five years) in the same church. We were married, we had just got two beautiful puppies – everything was pretty much as it was supposed to be. Swee and I had known each other for a long time before we were married (I had known her since I was nine and she was sixteen), so we felt it was the perfect time to have the children we were both more than ready for; the perfect combination of the best of both of us.

And there came the bump in the road. It turns out that getting pregnant just when you want to is nowhere near as straightforward as you might expect. Suddenly life felt as if it was completely out of our control as month by month went by with no signs of the planned-for and expected pregnancy.

Next came IVF, and that didn't work as we had hoped. Swee was forty-three by this point. At this age the chances of successful IVF drop considerably. We knew this, but we thought we had to give it a chance. We were referred to the local clinic and Swee started to take the required hormones to produce more eggs. These hormones are strong and affect people in all sorts of different ways. It was not a good experience for Swee. They really played havoc with her mental health, making her feel very paranoid about things happening around her. But she was determined to continue so that we could have a good harvest of eggs for the first round of IVF.

Then, a week before we were due to go to the clinic, we had a letter. It said that there had been cutbacks, and that, due to the low probability of us achieving a successful pregnancy, they would no longer treat us. This news was heartbreaking. There was nowhere else for us to go – we couldn't afford to pay for the treatment ourselves. That was the end of the road.

Looking back now, I am amazed at how resilient we stayed through all of this. Swee had faced the possibility of motherhood, however small; she had endured hormone treatment with all of its unpleasant side effects; and now suddenly, with no warning, the road was blocked. But we just picked ourselves up and started down the next road: adoption.

By this time we had already been considering adoption. My mother was adopted (more of that later), so we had a positive example of how well it can work, and as we were older (I was thirty-seven and Swee was forty-three) we were not necessarily looking to adopt a baby – in fact we had already decided that we would be very happy to take an older child or children. So we phoned our local adoption agency and started the process.

The adoption process

The adoption process is never an easy route. It would be easy here to criticise social workers – actually, I have a great deal of respect for many social workers and the extraordinarily hard job that they do. However, it is fair to say that we were let down badly by one of ours on several occasions.

I'm sure that the process is designed to put you off the idea of adopting. There is a good deal of sense in that in many cases. Adoption is also not that common. According to statistics published by Adoption UK in November 2022, 'There were 2,950 children adopted in the year 2022, falling from a peak of 5,360 in 2015… This sits against a backdrop of a rise in the number of children being placed into the care of local authorities – up by 2% in 2022, to an all-time high of 82,710.' Adoption is only considered once it has become clear that the child cannot remain with their parents or another family member.

The children who are available for adoption rarely come to you with no issues. Almost all of them will have suffered some form of abuse, even if that is only down to neglect and the fact that their birth parents are not able to look after them sufficiently. This situation is very different to that in the first half of the twentieth century, before effective birth control and when there were many more babies given up for adoption because of the stigma of being an unmarried mother. And if you do adopt a baby, they may well be suffering from foetal alcohol syndrome, or effects of drug abuse during pregnancy, which can have a profound effect on their future development.

The first issue that you will be asked to consider is if you are emotionally ready to adopt. For most people, adoption will not have been the original plan to have children. Nowadays many couples will have also tried fertility treatment before they consider adoption. All of this will have taken an emotional toll on the couple, and it is very important to come to terms with all of that – to mourn the fact that you will not have your own biological children – before you can be ready to help and love an adopted child. We found that working through that sense of loss is useful to help empathise with the sense of loss that your adopted child will have. All adopted children have experienced loss, even if it is just being taken away from their birth family.

The approval process will explore all aspects of your lives as individuals and as a couple. It will look at past relationships, how your relationship works now, what experience you have of being with children, what support you have around you to help with this life-changing decision. You have to be prepared for the fact that the process will be incredibly intrusive and just go with it. It is a hard time to go through, as you will be acutely aware that the social worker asking you questions will be writing a report at the end of all of this and deciding whether to recommend you or not. The process is also trying to ensure that potential abusers are weeded out of the system – it is a sad truth that adoption and fostering is a potential way for abusers to get access to children. There have been cases reported where children in care have been further abused by their carers – again betrayed by the people they are supposed to be able to trust the most. This was one of the reasons that Operation Acorne was set up in July 2017 to look at the failings in a number of agencies.

So, after going along to an introductory presentation and filling out a number of long forms about ourselves, we had our first meeting with our designated social worker, who almost at the beginning of the conversation announced that we would be very unlikely to be approved for adoption as we were too overweight. Despite any positive aspects about what we were able to offer to any children, we would never be considered. We were encouraged to take some months to lose weight before continuing with the process.

So, the diet started. Anyone who has been overweight at any time in their life will know how difficult it can be. The secret is to have a compelling goal (potentially becoming adoptive parents was perfect for that), and to find a diet that suits your body. I went full Atkins: loads of salads, vegetables and protein. Swee was always much better with calorie counting. It was tough, but over several months we began to see some changes. We both managed to lose several stone. I wouldn't say that it was the best way to lose weight, but we were keen to show our commitment so that we could begin the adoption journey.

We had ticked the box of losing a considerable amount of weight – enough for the agency to start the process proper. The next nine months consisted of many meetings with our social worker, both as a couple and individually. We went on training days with other prospective parents. References were written for us by family, friends and their children. We reflected on the number, age and sex of children we would consider. Finally, a report was written and we were invited to attend a panel to seek approval.

The panel meeting took place in Aldershot, about forty miles from where I live. The process was gruelling and intimidating. A group of six or seven people (made up of independent social workers, experienced adopters, medical advisers, and adult adoptees) are there to question you and your social workers before they decide to recommend you or not as potential adopters. In that meeting you just want to make the best impression in a short time, and to ensure that the panel really gets to know you and your motivations. Despite the stress, I was amazed by how eloquent Swee and I were able to be.

To give some context, Ofsted statistics published in November 2022 showed that of the more than 25,380 couples and individuals who made enquiries about adopting in the year to March 2022, just 4,145 went on to make an application, and only 3,048 were approved as adoptive parents. Although these are frightening statistics, by the time you make it to panel, it is hoped that the approval should be forthcoming. You hope you would have been rejected by then if you were going to be.

The panel asks all sorts of questions. No stone is left unturned – why do you want to adopt, what is your support network like (this is essential), do you have any experience of childcare, what is your ethnic background, why did you choose that particular age range, can you fit children into your lives, and so on. And of course, in our case, we had the further questions about our weight and our lifestyles.

One detail I do remember clearly is the place where we waited for our meeting with the panel. It was like a cupboard with a window. There wasn't much room for more than a small table, a couple of chairs, and a very large plate of chocolate biscuits. We had to wait for some time as the beginning of the panel meeting was taken up by our social worker presenting our case and being questioned by the panel. When, later, we were asked about our lifestyle and diet, I couldn't help but make the point that we did always try to make healthy choices, and that didn't include large plates of chocolate biscuits. I joked that we were suspicious that there were hidden cameras in the waiting area, and that they were testing us. Luckily, the panel appreciated the comment and it did lighten the atmosphere.

The process makes you question everything you thought you knew about yourself and what you want in your life and from your relationships. It is very hard – but it is the least these children deserve.

Following the panel meeting we then had to wait some weeks before we knew whether we had been successful or not. The news finally came by phone call as we were standing in front of a waterfall in Norway while we were on a cruise of the fjords, having escaped to clear our heads and try not to sit at home and stew while we waited. We had been approved to adopt one or two children up to the age of eight. That was it – our lives could now move forward again.

The matching process: finding Mac

There is a huge sense of relief once you have been approved as adoptive parents. It is a very bizarre and liminal time: standing on the edge of becoming a family at last, but not really sure when that will be. Once you have been approved, your details will be considered by your agency (in our case Hampshire County Council) every time they have a child in need of adoption. There is no way of knowing how long this stage will take. As we had made the decision to take an older child, it was a fair assumption that we might not have to wait too long as fewer people are willing to consider older children.

However, the months went by and there was no news. We had been considered a few times, but for various reasons we had come second to other couples. It always seems hard to believe that you are not matched more quickly. The news is always full of stories saying that there are not enough parents for the available children – but the truth is that counties like Hampshire have more potential adoptive parents than available children.

After a few months, your details are shared with other agencies. There are also other ways for matching to occur. Sometimes there are 'open evenings', normally held in school halls in my experience, where children's details are shared by the relevant social workers. It is a bit like a bizarre form of speed dating where you go around to the various agencies and see what they have on offer.

There is also a magazine called *Children Who Wait*, which publishes pictures and details of children who have been difficult to place – normally because of complex needs, because they are part of a large sibling group, or because of their ethnic mix or their age. Swee and I used to read this publication every month. We would read it separately and highlight any children about whom we might consider finding out more. If we agreed, then we would contact the relevant agency to get more details. We were fairly open about whether to adopt boys or girls. I think Swee had a slight preference for a girl, but I didn't mind. Older boys tend to find it harder to get adoptive placements – it seems that girls tend to be easier to place.

One day, about a year or so after our approval, I remember clearly seeing, as I was reading the magazine, a picture of a seven-year-old boy. He looked very happy swinging on a swing with wellies on his feet that were far too large for him. His name was Mac.

Soon after, we had a review meeting with our social workers to consider why we were not being matched and if there was anything that we needed to consider changing. Our social worker came along with her manager. It turned out that, in our case, many mistakes had been made: we had not been put onto the national register as promised, and one of our social workers had written down our details incorrectly, so the group of children for whom we were being considered was hopelessly narrow. I can still remember now the upset and frustration I felt – we had reached the point where we were about to give up on the idea of adoption and try to move on with our lives, and it turned out that the agency had messed up our case. All I wanted was to get those people out of my house – but before they left, the manager mentioned that she had the details of a boy who she thought was perfect for us, and that she hoped we would consider him. We agreed that she would leave the details and we would consider them and get back to her.

After they left, we were exhausted emotionally. We just didn't know if we could carry on with this process any longer. Maybe it was time to accept that we were not going to have children – we would fill our house with dogs and cats instead and make the most of our nephews, nieces and godchildren. We would look to enjoy our lives and move on from the dream of having a family.

I was so frustrated and angry that it wasn't until the next day that we opened the details that had been left with us. Of course, those details were Mac's. The more we read about him, the more we felt he was ideal for us. The more we read about the difficult start he'd had, the more we were sure that we would be able to help him. The more we read and the more we looked at his picture, the more we could imagine him as our son. We rang the agency, and the process started.

There is one thing I remember clearly from our matching panel that was very significant for me. It was very clear that we were Mac's last chance to have a family of his own and to be adopted, and I remember being asked how I felt about it. The answer was simple: Mac was our last chance to be parents, so we were in exactly the same position. It was so clear to me and to Swee that this was meant to be – we were somehow destined to be Mac's parents and it was something we couldn't wait to do.

After all of this time we had found our son – we had found Mac.

Chapter 3

14 November 2008

The introductions were complete and had gone well, and finally a date was set for Mac to move in. Just before this, Swee and I went on a long-planned holiday with my parents, sister and brother-in-law: a cruise to the Mediterranean that was to be our last adult holiday for some time.

Before we left, we went to see Mac to explain that we would be away and to assure him that we would be back. One of the most difficult issues for Mac was that he had been let down too many times: when adults said they would come to get him, it often didn't happen. One of the reasons he had finally been removed from his parents was that he had been left at school when his mother had gone away with his brother and not come to pick Mac up. This was the worst example of his being left somewhere and having to wait to be picked up – or, in this case, not being picked up at all. His attendance at school was also 'hit-and-miss'. By the time he was taken into care at the age of five, he had already missed more than half of his expected school time, meaning he'd missed some fundamental parts of his early learning. Most children instinctively trust the people around them until they are proved wrong. However, for adopted children it is common that their trust has been abused so many times that they tend not to trust until that trust has been built up. We were concerned that a fortnight would be a long time for Mac not to see us – as a young eight-year-old he still found the concept of time difficult. So we wrote him a number of letters and gave them to Sue and Mark to give to him at certain points during those two weeks to ensure that Mac felt that we were in touch and would be coming back.

Once we were back, we quickly went to see Mac with presents of a cuddly dog from us, a Barcelona football shirt from my sister, and plenty of sweets. Then Sue and Mark came over with Mac for Bonfire Night. The village always had a huge bonfire and firework display with hot dogs and baked potatoes. We had a great time, and we sensed that Mac was sad to leave that evening – he really was ready to move in.

The next time we were to meet was a week or so later, on moving-in day.

When we'd moved to the village a few years ago, Swee had very happily left her job working for the Medical Research Council. She'd enjoyed working in a few roles in the village, getting to meet everyone and to settle into the community. By the time we were ready to adopt Mac, Swee had worked for several years as a receptionist and administrator at our local GP's surgery. When you adopt, it is expected that one of the parents will be at home for an extended period of time, even if the child is of school age, to help the child get some feeling of permanence and to begin to feel part of the family. So Swee left her job to look after Mac.

I worked as head of policy at the Financial Services Authority, the UK's financial regulator. I loved my job, but it was very busy, and it did mean that I worked long days with a long commute from Hampshire to Canary Wharf every day. I would normally leave home at 5.30am and not be back until 7.30pm. However, I was entitled to take statutory adoption leave, which was enhanced to six weeks by my employer. At the time I was nervous about being away from work for so long. It was still unusual then (even in 2008) for men to take leave for childcare reasons, and it seemed like so long to be away. I was worried about how it might affect my career – would my department get used to me not being around? Would I be overlooked for good opportunities because I wasn't there (after all, 'out of sight, out of mind')?

I have to say, I am forever grateful to my director at the time, Paul. I had a great working relationship with him, and had said to him that although I was on adoption leave, I would be available to talk and could even pop in if necessary. Now, anyone who has worked with Paul will know that he has many impressive qualities, but his sense of pastoral care was not always top of the list! But he provided the best example of leadership that I can remember. He told me that I should forget work for the six weeks and concentrate on my new family. In fact, he went as far as to say that he would be angry if I did get in touch.

"When I get to the Pearly Gates, I don't want St Peter to blame me for you not bonding properly with your son," he said.

It was the kindest thing he could have done. He gave me the permission I needed to concentrate on my new life for six weeks without the daily distraction and stresses of work.

It was the morning of Friday 14 November 2008 – the first of my adoption leave. The timing of the adoption leave was going to work perfectly as it took me through to the week after Christmas.

I can't remember much about that morning. I think we were in a bit of a daze, making sure that everything was ready for Mac, but with everything feeling a little unreal. From today, that was it: he would be moving in and we would begin the journey to becoming a perfect unit – a new family.

Mid morning, Sue and Mark turned up with Mac, and Denise was also there. They unpacked the car and brought in three small boxes and a small suitcase with all of his stuff, which we took up to the bedroom.

We had been working up to this point for a few weeks, and Sue and Mark had been allowing us to spend longer and longer times with Mac. He had always had it explained to him that his time with them would be temporary, even though it did last for just over a year, and he knew that he would have to say goodbye at some point. By now, Mac had been in care for over three years, and had lived in several homes – he had got very used to saying goodbye to people. Sue and Mark purposely didn't stay long and waved goodbye before leaving us to it. (We would be seeing Denise again soon, as the social worker visits frequently to begin with to make sure everything is going well.) Mac took all of this in his stride. I did feel, however, that he sensed that this time was different. I think he sensed that this was it – this was his chance to really make a family and a permanent home for himself.

We helped Mac to unpack his things. There were already a few bits and pieces in his bedroom: some cuddly toys that we had accumulated together during visits, and some games. We also had a stained-glass rocket that Swee had found while away for a few days with her parents just after we had been matched with Mac (this hung against the window), and a few pictures on the walls. We had not done much more to the room, because we'd promised Mac that he could help decide how he wanted his bedroom decorated. He had some pictures that he wanted to put up – a particular favourite being his *Lord of the Rings* poster. Mac loved *The Lord of the Rings* and could watch it time and time again. One of his prized possessions was a cushion with his favourite character, Orlando Bloom as Legolas, which we placed on his bed. Then we went downstairs to sit down and have some lunch together and decide what we were going to do for the rest of the day.

That first day was pretty daunting. Swee and I had spent lots of time with our siblings' and friends' children, but now it was down to us. This relative stranger had come to live in our house, had come to be our son, and we wanted to make everything special and perfect. But how would we fill our time? What would we actually do to keep him entertained?

When you're adopting the situation is made even more difficult. You are advised to keep other people away as much as possible, even though as new parents you naturally want to have everyone round to be introduced to the new addition to your family. But of course, for the child that can be particularly daunting, so for the first few days it was just the three of us. We did say hello to a few people in passing – our next-door neighbours had similar-aged children and were keen to say hello.

Of course, we had thought about how we wanted things to be. We wanted to make sure that we integrated Mac into our lives as much as possible – if we needed to go shopping, we would take him with us and try to make the trip enjoyable; if we had things to do around the house, we would get him to help.

We decided to pop to the local supermarket. Although we had already stocked up on food, we wanted to see if there were any particular things that Mac would like to make him feel more at home. We had some idea of the things he liked from talking to Sue and Mark, and from the early visits Mac had made to stay with us before he moved in permanently. It was a way to make the day as normal as possible. It would have been easy to do lots of exciting things on the first day, but we were keen that Mac should fall into normal daily life with us.

So off we went, and for the first time we negotiated a supermarket with an eight-year-old in tow. So many things were different: strapping him into his booster seat in the car (he was just a little too short not to have one at that point); parking in the parent-and-child spot; walking around a supermarket trying to look like we weren't complete novices and this wasn't some unfamiliar child who had just walked into our lives!

It was an opportunity for Mac to identify some of his 'go-to' treats. Any type of milkshake was always very popular – whether it was the thick ones that are already made up, or just a few spoons of Nesquik in some milk. He loved making his own milkshakes, mixing different flavours to see how they turned out. Super Noodles were another favourite – a packet of Super Noodles always satisfied his hunger, particularly when he was in the middle of a growth spurt. Mac did like sweets, but his favourite flavour was definitely mint. He also liked chocolate and marshmallows – a hot chocolate with lots of marshmallows on top was his idea of heaven. And this love of mint and chocolate came together in mint choc chip ice cream. Mac had no great love of fruit at that point, but he was very happy to eat vegetables. Actually, what he loved most was a proper home-cooked meal. Swee's mince was legendary, and if Mac smelt it cooking on the hob, he knew there was going to be 'pesgetti' (his name for spaghetti) for tea. On an evening like that, he couldn't be happier. Somehow he realised the love and care that goes into cooking for your family, and that made him feel loved and wanted.

Once we came back from shopping, Mac and I went for a walk around the village, and over to the recreation ground and playground. We are lucky here to have really good facilities for our younger children, and Mac loved to play on the swings and the slide and the bouncy horse. Of course, what he was missing and craving was company of other children. He knew in his heart that he shouldn't be an only child; he shouldn't have to put up with just playing in the playground with me – he had a younger brother living in another home, and he felt that loss keenly. Although he would continue to have contact every six weeks or so, he wouldn't get to be the big brother on a day-to-day basis as he should.

As we sat on the bench in the playground eating a mint choc chip Cornetto (even though it was November!), he started to talk about wanting to make friends. He was very much looking forward to starting at the village school so that he could meet other children of his age and make the sorts of friendships he had dreamed about. Mac had been going to school while he was living with Sue and Mark, but friendships were hard to establish as he was never sure when he might have to move on. As he had moved around so many times in his eight years, and missed a great deal of school, Mac had lost out on the opportunity to make real friends and understand how friendships work. All of that was to come. Of course, in the same way that, as adults dreaming of having a family, Swee and I had built up in our minds an image of what being a family would be like, adopted children do exactly the same thing. They can have an idealised view of how things are going to be, and it is your job as adults to help them to negotiate the reality.

When we got home, there was a surprise waiting for Mac. One of our friends makes wonderful cakes, and she had kindly made a 'welcome home' chocolate cake and gifted him £20. Mac was stunned – I still have a picture of him looking lovingly at the cake and holding up the £20 note, smiling.

Finally, the evening came. As it was a special day for all of us, and a Friday night, we decided we would have a treat and get fish and chips. Mac and I went off to the local chippy to get our tea: cod and chips for Swee, and battered sausage and chips for me and Mac. (Mac and I shared a dislike of fish.) We sat at our table and ate up the chips and had a nice chat about what we would do over the next few days.

The 14 November 2008 was a special night for another reason: the annual *Children in Need* telethon was on the TV. We all snuggled up together on the sofa, watching our favourite TV stars doing silly things with the legendary Terry Wogan holding everything together. Mac was cuddled up next to me and I could feel him relaxing and getting tired and ready for bed after a very busy and eventful day. There were lots of short films showing some of the children who had been helped by the charity and how the money had made a difference.

As he was watching the TV, Mac said, "That's a bit like me. I used to be a children [sic] in need, but I'm not any more now I have come to live here."

They say from the mouths of babes! To be honest Swee and I were pretty emotional anyway, but this quickly brought a tear to the eye.

"That's right, Mac," I said.

From that day, Children in Need was our favourite charity. Mac always loved the opportunity to get involved at school and to help raise as much money as possible. He easily identified with the plight of the children he saw on the TV – there was a real sense of emotional intelligence and empathy with them.

It was soon time for a bath and bed. Mac was used to this as his routine, and it was a routine we were glad to continue. Mac had a lovely warm bath with lots of bubbles and then he got into his pyjamas and into bed. I sat next to his bed and read him a story – I had decided to work through the *Mr. Men* books (we had the complete set that had belonged to my nephews). We looked at the pictures together and followed the words of *Mr. Happy*.

Finally, we added something to bedtime. On a previous visit, we had given Mac a picture with an angel and a prayer on it. The prayer was one that I had been taught by my godfather when I was young, and we had passed it on to several of our godchildren over the years. It's a lovely prayer to say with a child at night-time and we wanted to work it into Mac's routine. It goes like this:

God is above me, my safety to keep,
Angels are watching and guarding my sleep,
The sweet stars are shining to keep away fear,
My mummy and daddy, I know, are quite near,
I'm loved and I'm happy,
My small heart is light,

Thank you for everything, dear God,
Goodnight.

We said this prayer every night and Mac would join in with the 'goodnight', but very soon learned the rest of the words himself. It was always a lovely way to calm him down and prepare him for sleep. Swee then came up and we both kissed him goodnight and he went off to sleep.

We went downstairs, pleased that we had got through the day and excited about everything that was to come. I stayed up to watch more of *Children in Need* to see how much was raised, and then followed Swee to bed. It was so nice to be able to check in on Mac on the way to bed and see that he was sleeping deeply, with a couple of cuddly toys clutched to his chest.

Chapter 4

The First Week

Becoming Mum and Dad

One of the things that most potential adoptive parents ask is "What will I be called?", especially if the child is older. Of course, they already have a birth mother and father, and so will already have someone that they want to call 'Mum and Dad'. I remember thinking that I didn't mind what Mac called me, as long as we were all happy. But of course, I was lying to myself. After such a long time trying to have a family, the desire to be called 'Dad' was very strong. The words 'Mum' and 'Dad' are more than just language – they signify the ultimate bond.

Up to this point we had been 'Richard and Swee' to Mac. (Although she was known as Swee to just about everyone, Swee's real name was Sunita. But when she was young, her cousin couldn't pronounce her name, so she'd gained the nickname 'Swee'Pea' after the character from *Popeye*. It stuck!) I wondered how the change to 'Mum and Dad' would be made. Would it be something that would happen over time, or would it happen more quickly?

Mac slept very well on the first night. I know Swee and I were both fairly restless, listening for him to see if he wanted anything, hoping he was happy. But the night was uneventful, and we all eventually got some sleep.

The next morning, Swee got up early to get breakfast ready. Mac woke up and came into our bedroom and jumped into bed as I was getting dressed. We started to have a pretty mundane conversation, with me asking how he'd slept and what he might like to do that day. Then I plunged in with the question I had been longing to ask.

"Do you think you might like to call me and Swee 'Mum and Dad' one day?"

"Yes," he said. And with that, he went to the top of the stairs and called downstairs to Swee, "You want to be my new mum. Can you get me some new pants as these ones are too tight?!" He was standing in a tight pair of Y-fronts.

Swee went off to the supermarket to buy many different styles of pants in what she thought was the right size, never having bought pants for an eight-year-old before.

From that moment Mac started calling us Mum and Dad, and never called us Richard and Swee again. I can still remember that day, and the first time I heard someone calling me Dad. It was something I had imagined for so long. It was something that I had ached for, and here was this beautiful, perfect, loving boy blessing me with that name. It's something I have never taken for granted.

Of course, the reality of adopted children is that they do have other parents. And if your child was adopted at an older age, they will have a relationship with them. We never forgot that, or criticised Mac's birth parents. We would always explain that they hadn't been able to look after him as they had got their priorities wrong, rather than going into any detail. As the child grows, they start to work more of it out for themselves and to understand their situation on a more mature level. We always referred to Mac's birth parents by their Christian names, so that if I was talking about his mum, he knew I was talking about Swee. Mac tended to refer to all four of us interchangeably as Mum and Dad, and it is amazing that it was never confusing for us as we were always able to understand which of us he was referring to. However, the same could not be said for when we were outside the house.

Swee and my sister, Sandra, had taken Mac to the archery club held in a local hall. It was something he had always wanted to try – probably due to his ongoing love of Robin Hood and Legolas from *The Lord of the Rings*. There was a good club locally that worked well with young beginners. Swee and Sandra were sat on the sidelines, talking to a few parents, while Mac was being shown how to fire the arrows.

He was doing quite well, when suddenly they overheard his conversation with the other youngsters. For some reason the subject must have got on to drugs, and Swee overheard him say, in a completely matter-of-fact way, "My mum is a drug addict."

Suddenly there was silence in the room as everyone turned to look at my wife.

At that point Mac said, "Oh! Not *that* mum. I'm adopted!"

Adopted children will get you into all sorts of scrapes that you might not be prepared for.

Lapland UK

So, back to our first few days together.

It had been decided that Mac should spend a few days at home with us before he started at the local primary school. (All children who have been in the care system, even after they have been adopted, get priority on school lists, so we had no problem getting into our local school, even though it was always very popular.) This was a chance for us all to bond and to start to settle into the rhythm of life as a new family.

As we'd known that this time was coming, we had done some planning to decide what we might do with the time. We wanted to do something memorable and start to make memories with Mac. As it was running up to Christmas we looked to see if there were Christmassy things that we could do together, and found that there was a new experience that was being laid on called Lapland UK, where you could get the chance for that 'Lapland and Father Christmas' experience without having to travel abroad. (Travel abroad was not something we could contemplate as we did not have parental control at this point and Mac did not have a passport. Full parental control does not come until the adoption order is made. Up until that point, which at the earliest is likely to be about six months, the council retains ultimate control – including in decisions over the child's healthcare. It is a strange time as a new family.) So, we booked tickets. With the tickets came an invitation to Mac from Father Christmas to come and visit him in 'Lapland'. We wanted to make it special, so on the Sunday morning after he arrived, we made sure that Mac found the invitation on top of the wood burner in our sitting room. He was so excited! He had visited Father Christmas once before, but he certainly hadn't travelled to Lapland.

The next day, we drove to the venue in Kent. This was quite a long drive, and added to the excitement and the impression that we were travelling a very long way. Mac always fell asleep in the car. As he woke up, we were just approaching the site.

We went up to the entrance. We were given a time slot to enter. Together with a number of parents and their children, we were taken by elves to the entrance to 'Lapland' and entered an enclosed area decorated as an enchanted wood. As we walked further the scenery became snowier, and it certainly made you feel as if it was getting colder. The elves explained that we were walking along a magic path that would take us all the way to Lapland. As we came out of the wood we came across a huge pair of gates and entered a winter wonderland full of snow and looking every bit as if we had come across Lapland.

There was loads to do. We visited real reindeer. Mac decorated gingerbread biscuits with Mother Christmas. We ate lunch in a dining room full of elves. We were able to buy lots of Christmas decorations and Christmas sweets. The highlight of the day was visiting Father Christmas. Before we went to see him, I went along to a special office where I was able to fill in a form with key details about Mac, so that Father Christmas would be able to recount them and keep the illusion real. Of course this was so difficult, as many of the questions were unanswerable: who was his best friend? What was his favourite thing to do? Mac was in a new home and I wasn't sure I could provide the right answers. So, I went up to the desk and explained Mac's situation. The organisers were fantastic and said they would explain everything.

We went into a waiting room and were collected by an elf who led us through a snowy wood to reach a wood cabin. We entered, and there was Father Christmas sitting on reindeer skins, ready to weave his magic. Mac was open-mouthed. Father Christmas related a few facts – knowing Mac's name; knowing the names of our dogs – and then he said the most precious thing.

"I know that you have just moved to live with these special people. I am sure you will be very happy. I know where you live and will make sure I deliver some special presents."

He handed over some presents to Mac: a copy of *The Night Before Christmas* and a beautiful cuddly toy in the shape of a husky puppy. We left the visit very happy.

There was one more thing that Mac wanted to do. There was a wonderful ice-skating rink and he was keen to try it out. Now, neither Swee nor I was any good at ice skating. I had once tried it and never been able to let go of the side – and Swee had had an experience just as bad! So we knew that we would be of no help, but we didn't want to disappoint him. With luck, the venue had thought about everything and there were special 'ice-skating elves' there to help the children who were not very proficient. Mac put on his skates and took to the ice. We were terrified that he was going to hurt himself. When a child first moves in with you, you do not have parental control – it still sits with social services, who visit a lot to see how things are going. We were so worried that he might fall over.

"We can't break him in the first week that he lives with us!" Swee said.

Of course, we shouldn't have worried. Mac was well looked after by the elf and had a great time skating on the ice.

After that, we were all tired and decided it was time to start the journey home. As soon as we started driving, Mac fell asleep again and slept the whole two-and-a-half-hour journey home. We finished the day by picking up his favourite pizza on the way back to the village.

That night we decided that it was time for Mac to write his Christmas list to Father Christmas. He wrote a modest list, and we put it on the wood burner where the invitation from Father Christmas had arrived. We left a drink and a cake for Father Christmas (we didn't have any mince pies yet), and Mac went to bed in the hope that Father Christmas would pick up his list. (Of course he did, and he also enjoyed the cake and the drink!)

We all slept well that night.

The last days before school

The next morning Mac came downstairs and checked on the wood burner (we had closed the door to the sitting room so it looked like no one had been in there) and announced to us that the letter had gone and that Father Christmas had also had the cake and drink.

We started to plan Mac's bedroom with him, asking what colour walls he would like and arranging bits of furniture. He had been given lots of books by our friends and family, so we ordered some bookshelves. We found a small hammock into which we were able to put all of the soft toys that people had bought for him. We made sure that there were plenty of pictures, and that it started to feel like *his* room and that he felt comfortable in it. We wanted to make sure that it was a place where he always felt safe; a sanctuary that he could retreat to when things were difficult.

Mac and I spent a lot of time together. Swee was getting everything ready for Christmas – writing cards to everyone and letting them know of our news and that Mac had moved in. We had made the conscious decision that I would spend as much time with Mac as I could during my adoption leave as we knew that

I would never get concentrated time with him like that again. After Christmas my long commute would resume. We made many trips to the recreation ground and the children's playground; kicking balls around, and me pushing Mac on the swing. Again and again, Mac talked about how excited he was to be starting school and to be able to make new friends. Certainly it was not the academic side of things that he was looking forward to, but the opportunity to mix with his own age group.

Just before Mac started school he had a session with his play therapist, Chris. He had spent a lot of time with Chris over the last couple of years – first to get him ready for his adoptive placement with his brother, and then to help him get over being taken away and split up from him. Chris was extremely fond of Mac and had helped him through key moments in his life. She was so pleased that he had found a placement that looked like it should work for him.

I remember Chris coming to visit us at the house for the first time and saying, "I love to get together with the children for some messy play so that we can help them come to terms with everything that is happening to them." (I have to say that I wasn't that keen on the idea of 'messy' play!)

Chris and Mac spent some time together painting, and we left them to it. It was important that Mac felt he could tell her anything he needed to without us overhearing. The session went well and Chris arranged to come back in a week or so to see how he was coping with his new school.

I have to be honest: I had been a little sceptical about the effectiveness of play therapy, and there were times when I was sure that Mac was 'playing the game' and saying what he thought they wanted to hear. Once, Chris left an orangutan glove puppet called

Charlie with us so that Mac could talk to him if he needed to. (The first thing Mac asked us to do was put Charlie in the wardrobe as he was terrified of it!)

But it was clear that Mac and Chris had a very special and close bond, and there is no doubt in my mind that it was partly her work with him that helped him to be ready, eager and able to settle into a new adoptive placement, so we will always be grateful for the work that she did with him. She and Mac's social worker, Denise, were effectively the only continuity that Mac had experienced in his life. They were important. But it was interesting to see that Mac began to need them much less as he transferred his trust to us. As he began to embrace his new life, he was keen to cast off those things that reminded him of the difficulties of the past.

The first few days had gone well. We were starting to fall into a pattern and it was clear that Mac was more than ready to start school. So on the Wednesday morning of 19 November 2008, just five days after he moved into our home, he started at St Mary Bourne Primary School.

Chapter 5

The Honeymoon Period (and Beyond!)

As part of the preparation for approval as adoptive parents, it is necessary to go on some training courses. This is a good opportunity to spend some time with people in the same position as you, and to have some concentrated time to get to grips with the sorts of things that you might face.

One of the things we were told is that it is usual for there to be a honeymoon period when a child first moves in with you for adoption. For a period of time, it is likely that the child is going to try as hard as possible to make sure that you like them and that you will want them to stay. This was certainly true of Mac. He was so keen to have a new family of his own that his behaviour was exemplary.

For the first couple of weeks everything went really well. But we knew this wasn't the real Mac. We knew he wasn't telling us everything. He didn't want to ask for anything, and so would say, "I thought you might like a biscuit", which was his way of saying that he would like a biscuit himself. But we managed to read through some of the code and he seemed very happy at home.

We quickly found the things that he needed to feel safe (helpfully prompted, in many cases, by Sue and Mark's tips to us). For much of Mac's childhood he had been short of food, or not been sure where the next meal would be coming from. So to be happy to go to bed, he always wanted to know that there was a glass of water and a packet of biscuits in his bedroom. Because of his early experiences with his birth parents, he was always worried when we dropped him off at school that we would not pick him up, so we always made sure that one of us was at the school in plenty of time and in the same place so that he could see us as soon as he was let out of the classroom.

Some things would send Mac into a meltdown for no apparent reason. He hated loud noises and shouting, and particularly hated it if someone knocked on the door too loudly. Eventually he told us that he had a memory of someone knocking down his birth parents' door with an axe and coming after his father. That memory always haunted him and sometimes appeared in his dreams. We also found out that Mac was terrified of what would happen if he broke something. If he dropped a cup or a plate, he would get really scared that he was going to be told off. We always made sure that we were very calm and explained to him that it didn't matter and was an accident, and that he was much more important than anything material. Adopted children often come with all of this baggage and it takes some time to unpack everything and start to help them overcome these memories – sometimes all you can do is help them live with it. We always encouraged Mac to talk to us about these things so that we could try to help him. Over time it is inevitable that memories will come out that you won't have been told about; that social workers could never had known. An important part of the role of an adoptive parent is to help your child deal with all of that.

We enjoyed the honeymoon period with Mac. Things were going so well. But we knew enough to know that this was going to change. Sure enough, after just two weeks the honeymoon period ended. Mac had decided to see where the boundaries really were.

Of course, most adopted children have very low self-esteem. They will have suffered so much neglect and rejection that they find it hard to trust or to really believe that anything is going to be permanent – after all, their experience so far is that nothing lasts forever. They have always had to move on. And whatever they have been told, they will think that all of that is their fault. Their behaviour starts to change as they look for the boundaries to see what they can actually get away with. I'm a great believer that all children need boundaries. They find safety in knowing how far they can push you, and that you care enough to react and to put rules in place. And as they grow, those boundaries will continue to be tested and you will make decisions about how they might change.

When you talk to people involved with children in the care system, they will often tell you that most looked-after children will push the boundaries as far as they can. I think Mac, in common with many in his position, wanted to push them as hard as he could because he found it hard to believe that we wouldn't change our minds and decide that we didn't want him – after all, that had happened to him in his last adoptive placement. Why should we be any different? So Swee and I were very clear with him about what was and wasn't acceptable. But we also made it clear that whatever he did, we would always love him and always want to be his parents.

That consistency was so important to keep to. But I can promise you that it was not always easy.

Bedtime

Mac was normally very good at going to bed. He enjoyed being in his bedroom. We had made sure that it was a comfortable place where he could always feel safe. We'd established a bedtime routine of a bubble bath (he always loved lovely smells and bubbles), going downstairs to say goodnight to Swee, followed by my reading him a bedtime story and saying his bedtime prayer. He would then snuggle down and go to sleep. I would normally come back up half an hour or so later to check that he was asleep. There's nothing better than seeing your child snuggled up in bed, sleeping soundly.

To begin with, this routine always worked, but one night, as the honeymoon period came to an end, Mac decided he wasn't going to go to bed. He sat cross-legged on the kitchen table and wouldn't budge! I wasn't really sure what to do next. I didn't want to get straight into punishments, so I made it clear that he had to go to bed and that I would sit at the kitchen table with him until he did as he had been told. Of course, I hadn't any further plan, and Mac was in a determined mood. We sat for what seemed like an eternity, and must have been an hour. I was insisting that he should go to bed or he would feel tired and grumpy in the morning, but he wasn't going anywhere. Not only was he not moving; he was being moody and rude.

"I bet you were never like this for Sue and Mark," I said.

"Yes, I was!" he retorted.

At a loss as to what I should do next, I decided to phone Sue and Mark to see if that might change the mood. Mac really didn't think I would, so I rang their number, hoping and praying that they were there. Mark answered the phone.

"Hi, Mark," I said. "It's Richard here. I'm afraid Mac is being very naughty tonight. He tells me he was like that at your house."

Mark played ball. "No," he said, "he was never rude to us."

I repeated this back to Mac, still sitting defiantly on the kitchen table, legs and arms crossed. "Would you like to talk to him?" I said.

At this point, Mac poked his tongue out at me! And with that, he picked up the phone, put his best voice on, and talked politely to Mark. I don't know what Mark said – I didn't ask – but it was enough to change the mood, and when he had finished on the phone, Mac stomped up the stairs and went to bed, and was soon asleep.

To be fair to Mac, he always woke up happy, whatever had happened the night before. It was often the evenings when he played up, usually because he was tired. It is not unusual for adopted and looked-after children to need more sleep – day-to-day life just tends to be more emotionally draining for them.

The other times when Mac would play up was if we had people round after he went to bed. He hated the feeling that he was missing out on something. One evening I was out and Swee had my sister round. Mac had seen Sandra when she arrived, and then went off to bed. But he couldn't resist coming down and, despite being told repeatedly, would not go back to bed. Eventually, after having tried several times, Swee said that she would shut the sitting-room door and he would just have to go off to bed. As she marched out of the sitting room, he caught hold of her top by the sleeve. As cool as you like, Swee managed to get herself out of her top, and Mac was left stranded with just her top in his hand. She shut the door and told him one more time to go to bed. Mac realised he had been outwitted and stomped upstairs, leaving my sister open-mouthed and my wife standing in just her bra. But she had won the battle and the boundary had been set.

It wasn't just us that Mac played up for at bedtimes. To be honest, we didn't leave him with anyone else very much. We felt it was important that he had consistency and knew that one of us was always around for him. But we knew it was also important for us as a couple to be able to go out and have other people babysit. The first time we went out, we asked my sister to babysit. We only went to the local pub, just a five-minute walk away, in case there were any problems. So, we went out and had a lovely evening. When we got back, all was quiet: Mac was asleep in bed and Sandra was watching the TV. It was a great relief that everything had gone swimmingly... However, not all was as it seemed. Mac had decided he was going to play a trick on his Aunty Sandra. He'd had a bath, they'd read a story, and he'd gone to bed happily. But he'd known that she would come up to check on him – so he'd hidden in the wardrobe. My sister had come upstairs and was beside herself. In the moment, she hadn't thought to look anywhere and was convinced she had lost him – what would she do and what would we say? Of course, she did then start looking around, and there he was, sitting quietly in the wardrobe, waiting for her to find him. He thought it was very funny – I'm not sure my sister was as amused!

One of the more surprising and endearing things that Mac did happened very quickly. Once he had gone to bed, the rule was that he was not allowed downstairs again. (This was a rule inherited from my childhood. My sister and I have strong memories of sometimes sitting on the landing, listening to the dinner parties downstairs, but never daring to venture down.) For us as new parents, we knew we needed that downtime to decompress and to have the opportunity to discuss how things were going. Things can move very quickly with an eight-year-old finding his feet and gaining confidence.

Sometimes we would hear Mac pottering around upstairs. We would leave him to it. We wanted him to feel comfortable once he had gone up to bed, and as long as he soon settled down, we tried not to interfere, as we knew this might prolong bedtime. The first time we heard him do this, he was going into our bedroom. When we went to bed ourselves we found a little note on one of our pillows. Mac's writing and spelling were not at all good at this point, but we were starting to get good at deciphering them, and he had written a note saying how happy he was and that he loved us. This was the first of many notes from Mac – sometimes to say sorry, or that he had had a good day, or just to tell us how he felt. It became a really important way for him to communicate with us. Eventually it stopped, but it did go on for a few years. I still have them all.

Working with social workers

One of the more difficult aspects at the beginning of an adoptive placement is that you still get lots of visits from social workers. They come to see how things are going, and will always talk to you and the child separately, just to make sure things are working out. I know that for many adoptive parents this is particularly stressful. As I mentioned earlier, we had some issues with our social worker as she had made many mistakes, especially after our approval. Although we had a good relationship with Mac's social worker, Denise, we were still keen to get to the date when the adoption had gone through and we would no longer be bothered by frequent visits. You cannot apply for the adoption order from the court until all sides are content that the placement is working. We were able to apply for the adoption order pretty quickly after just a few months, but it was still not made until six months after Mac had moved in.

Having spoken to a number of people involved with children in care, we were told that those kids who have been in care for some time know how to work the system. They get pretty clever at knowing what to say to their social worker – after all, you have to remember that everything is always done in the best interests of the child. That can make the potential parents feel pretty vulnerable at times. Of course, everyone is trying to pull in the same direction, but I don't think any parent welcomes someone coming in to question why they handled a situation in a particular way.

On the whole, we had a good relationship with our social worker. She had worked with Mac and his family for a long time. She was due to retire, and was pleased that she would be able to see Mac into a stable placement before she finally finished work – he was one of her two last cases.

Mac only got us into difficulties once. I can't even remember why the situation occurred. It had been one of Mac's difficult bedtimes. He had a small book that had the telephone numbers of important people in it. It was something he had so that he knew that if he wanted to get in touch with them, he would have their number. One of the numbers was that of a couple who had provided respite foster care for him when he was with Sue and Mark, and they were on holiday. They had also been foster carers for him and his brother when they were first placed into care. They had similar-aged children, and he had happy memories of his time with them. There had been a possibility that he might stay with them, but this would not have been adoption, but long-term fostering. (With long-term fostering, the child continues to be in the care of the state, and the state continues to pay the foster carers.) Mac really wanted to be adopted, to have a mum and dad of his own like his younger brother had, so it was decided that an adoption placement was still in his best interests. However, understandably Mac was still very fond of them.

On this particular evening, Mac had gone up to bed, gone into our bedroom, and phoned this couple to say that he was not happy (which was true: he had just been told off!). Of course, he didn't give her any of the context and she immediately phoned the duty social worker. As we had never been introduced, she didn't know us and didn't have any contact details for us. While I understand her actions, it was disappointing that she hadn't tried to contact us in any other way.

The next day, our social worker arrived to confront us with this, and to talk to Mac about it. To be fair to Denise, she was fairly sure that everything was OK, but she had to take this seriously in case Mac really was unhappy and things were not working out well. It was a total surprise to us as we had no idea that all of this had been going on. Thankfully, all of this was easy to explain. Mac was very contrite. It was close to Christmas, so we encouraged him to call the foster carers again, so that he could wish them a happy Christmas and have a better conversation and let them know that he was happy and that things were going well.

In fact, we did find that social workers could be useful sources of advice. As the weeks went by Mac was getting increasingly angry, and we wanted to find ways to help him and us to deal with it. We spoke to one specialist social worker who provided us with some great tips. The first one was about control – in fact, most of the issues Mac had were around control and who should have it. It is very easy as parents to think that you must always be the ones in control – and it is important to be in overall control. But many adoptive children will have spent their whole lives with no sense of control at all; with their chaotic lives completely out of their control and many things happening around them that make them feel unhappy or unsafe. So, we found that we needed to give Mac an element of control. I have to say it was one of the hardest things that we had to learn. One suggestion was to give him a couple of choices and then let him go with the one he wanted, rather than just telling him how something was going to be. It could be simple things like what to have for dinner, or whether to go to the cinema or soft play; but in this way, he would get the ability to make a choice (albeit a limited one), which gave him a sense of control. And we still retained ultimate control where needed by setting up the choices. We got better and better at it – and as we did, things did become easier, and it helped Mac learn to make choices.

Another tip that I would like to pass on was a way to help with anger. With adopted children (and others in care), it is often the case that they cannot help getting angry – they get to a point where they just cannot control it any more. However much you tell them to calm down, the wiring in their brains will not let them do it. Mac used to know this was happening and would warn us and tell us to leave him alone. One of his educational psychologists gave us the best trick ever to help him with these episodes of anger. As he got to that point (and we got better at recognising when it was happening), we asked him to do simple sums – two plus two; three plus three – making sure they were straightforward. Making him concentrate on something logical used a different part of his brain: the logical part. The first time we did this, we were pretty sceptical, but as soon as he started giving us the answers, it was possible to see him calming down and becoming able to regain control of his emotions. It sounds ridiculous, but I promise it works – even in the middle of pretty ferocious temper tantrums.

Mac also went through a spate of bad dreams, and we wanted a way to help him with it. This is the advice we were given: give him a pair of magic boots. For Mac, the nightmare normally involved someone nasty chasing him. So, as he was falling asleep, we would tell him he had a pair of magic boots, and that if anyone chased him in his dream, he could reach for them and he would be able to get away. Again, it's a simple idea but like so many simple ideas, it works.

We found so much of the advice and support helpful – the professionals have seen so much of this before that they can be a useful source of help when you need it. But that doesn't mean that they were always right.

We were warned that we should never get into bed with Mac. I think the feeling was that this would leave us vulnerable if Mac wanted to say something about us and accuse us falsely. And while I can see the sense in that, sometimes for the sake of your child you have to follow your instincts. Most mornings at the weekends, Mac would jump into bed with us (luckily we had a very large bed!). He loved the contact and would love to play tickling games. Mac would regress and act much younger than his years. What you often find with adopted children is that they will display younger behaviour, trying to fill the gaps of things they missed out on. He particularly wanted to be close to Swee as his mum. This culminated in the best and most heartfelt comment that he ever gave her: "I wish that I had come out of your tummy."

Adopted children get you into difficult situations

You have to be ready for all sorts of difficult situations as an adoptive parent. I've already mentioned the embarrassment that Swee faced when she took Mac to archery!

What you will find is that most people want to know what happened to your child – they want to know their story. But you have to remember that the story is the child's to tell – it is something between you and them, and you share it sparingly and only if absolutely necessary (e.g. with health professionals and teachers). Even then, you need to think carefully about how much they need to know. This can get difficult with friends and acquaintances – those who really care about you will understand, but many don't. There is a morbid fascination with what might have gone on in your child's life before. Of course, the problem with there being a vacuum of information is that some people will choose to fill it with assumptions and misinformation. This can lead to some awkward situations, and all I can say is that your first loyalty is always to your child, and you soon find out who your real friends are.

We did find that many parents were happy for Mac to take the blame for things he didn't do – in fact, Mac was normally happy to take the blame himself, maybe seeing it as an opportunity to endear himself to his peers. Swee had some of the most difficult interactions, and shares them later in this book.

You also learn how to deal with your child's tantrums by trial and error. Fairly early on, Mac was in a foul mood in his bedroom. I went upstairs and very calmly sat on his bed as he started to throw all of his soft toys around. Figuring that this wasn't too dangerous, I decided to call his bluff and suggest that he kick them around as well (thinking I was being a marvellous parent and outwitting him!). He went to kick one teddy bear really hard, but misjudged and kicked the floor – I could hear the crunch of his foot. Luckily our local GP is very close by and she was happy to see him straight away (it was just before they shut the surgery for the night). I explained what had happened – our GP was fully aware of our situation as Swee had worked there for a long time in reception, so they had lived through the whole process with us. She examined Mac's foot and declared that nothing was broken; just badly bruised. Lots of limping went on for a few days – even if it wasn't always the same foot! But the most important thing that Mac learned was that we cared enough to take him to the doctor when he was hurt.

My early memories

One of the first things I can remember with Mac is teaching him about jokes. Mac had the most fantastic laugh: it rang out with complete abandon, like a peal of bells. I loved to see him laugh – tickling him always worked a treat. If you tickled him, he could barely stand it, but he didn't want you to stop. He would laugh and laugh. Like most kids he wanted to learn how to tell jokes – though he was dreadful at it! It took a while for him to fully understand the concept. Making him laugh was easy: as long as it had a bottom or a fart in the joke it was a sure-fire winner. However, he had a favourite joke which is still one of my favourites today:

Question: *What do you call a monkey with a bomb?*
Answer: *A baboom!*

Mac and I loved to go to the cinema together. The first film we went to was called *Hotel for Dogs*. It was a charming story, but very soon I started to get worried. I hadn't done my homework to find out the main plot, and the two children involved were in foster care and trying not to be split up – exactly what had happened to Mac and his brother. I was sitting there, terrified that it might upset him.

But as ever, Mac surprised me and said, in a matter-of-fact way, "That's a bit like me, isn't it?"

And that was it. It's amazing how many children's films have the premise of adoption or fostering and children not being with their parents. Anyway, enough to say that *Hotel for Dogs* remains a firm family favourite.

Chapter 6

Primary School

Mac was very keen to start at school. For most of us, starting at a new school is pretty daunting, but Mac had done this at least four times already in his short life – for him it was just a normal part of the changes he had exprcienced. The important thing for him was that it provided access to other children and an opportunity to make friends.

He had also made some important decisions for himself. He had not been adopted at this point, so his surname had not legally changed. He sensibly asked if he could be known as Mac Sutcliffe – he didn't want to have to change his name later, and I think he was making a break from his past.

We are very lucky in our village as we have an outstanding school. It is big enough to have enough children (and therefore funding) to be viable, but still small enough for all of the children to be known really well by all of the teachers. There is a positive warm family atmosphere and we were very happy that Mac was to become a part of that. We were also lucky that the school had good experience of looked-after children, so Mac was not a novelty.

Before Mac moved in, the teachers from his last school were able to meet up with the head of our village school. It was such a good opportunity to make the transfer as successful as possible. Mac had missed a great deal of school in his early life: he had hardly been at school for 50% of the time in reception and year one. This meant that he had missed out on all of the basics – particularly phonics – so his reading and writing were way behind his peers'. Of course, he had also missed out on the social learning: how to make friends with other children. All of this, together with the level of anger that Mac felt, meant that school was not going to be that easy to start with. We knew that this was something that we would be tackling together.

Your relationship with your child's school is crucial as an adoptive parent. You need to work seamlessly with the school so that issues can be sorted. But you also need to advocate for your child when you think things are not happening in the way that you think they should.

One thing we were very keen on was that Mac should not acquire lots of labels. I have seen some adoptive parents look for explanations for all sorts of behaviours in their children. Of course, sometimes this is very important: if you need to have your child 'statemented' to get the help that they need, or if there are particular issues that need specific help. But we didn't think that saddling Mac with a collection of labels would help him at all. It was fairly clear to us that his issues could be tracked back to the fact that he had missed out on some of the real basics early on in life. There was no developmental delay due to any physical problems, so we were keen to work to 'normalise' Mac and to help him fill in the gaps.

Mac's birthday was in August, so he was one of the youngest in his year. It had been decided that since he had missed so much school, he should be held back a year – it was obvious that he would not be able to cope in his 'correct' school year. So Mac was to join year three – after all, he was only two weeks older than the oldest in this class.

His first day came and he happily got dressed in his new uniform and we took him to school. We took him up to meet the head. She greeted us all and then took him off to his classroom to meet his new classmates and teacher. We went home, not sure what to do with the time, waiting anxiously to pick him up that afternoon and find out how the day had gone.

It is always difficult starting at a new school when the other children are already established. Although Mac was desperate to make friends, he wasn't that good at it. He had missed out so much on his early schooling that he didn't understand some of the nuances of making friends. He also hadn't built up the resistance to falling out with friends: a lesson that most had already learned was that sometimes even the best of friends do not always get along.

There was a particularly troubled boy in his year. He behaved badly, and Mac and he had a bit of a love–hate relationship. Very early on, there was an incident in Mac's classroom. Someone had crept in during one of the breaks and written all over the walls and destroyed some of the other children's artwork. Mac had immediately owned up to it. Of course, as new parents, you are still getting to know your child and it is difficult to judge why they do certain things. But something didn't seem right. Luckily Mac's class teacher was very astute and was pretty sure that Mac had nothing to do with the incident. She pursued the matter over a few days and finally managed to get the other boy to admit that it had been him and Mac had had nothing to do with it. A girl had also been involved, and confirmed that it was not Mac. We were so grateful to Mac's teachers – they were getting to know him and followed their instincts. We sat down with Mac to ask why he had taken the blame.

"Well, I knew that unless someone owned up, the whole class was going to get into trouble. So, I thought it was best for me to own up. I knew the other boy wouldn't and I didn't want everyone else to be told off." On some level, he was doing it for the good of others and to be liked. I think his self-esteem was still so low that he also felt he deserved to be the one in trouble.

This is not to say that Mac didn't get into his own share of trouble. He was still dealing with a lot of anger issues and was prone to losing his temper from time to time. Also, as he struggled with a lot of schoolwork, he could often be quite distracting. When the class first came in in the morning, they were expected to settle down and get on with the task that was written on the board. Mac could never settle down, and would wander round the classroom, distracting everyone else.

When he was getting frustrated, particularly during playtime, one of the teaching assistants, Trish, would often walk around with him. Trish is a family friend – she has children the same age as my nephews and I have known her since I first moved to the village at the age of twelve. She was so good to Mac, and would often take him off and help him to calm down. I think she was instrumental in teaching him strategies to help when he did get frustrated in school.

But try as he might, friendships were difficult for Mac. There was already a tight-knit group of boys in his year. They were pretty friendly and patient, but Mac could be difficult. The truth is that he found it much better to be around adults. As he'd moved so much in his life, he was very good at being endearing around adults and getting them to like him – he was charming. But this behaviour did not translate into making friends with peers.

He was more successful at making friends with girls. At his best Mac was gentle and kind, and I think the girls were interested in this new, good-looking boy who was now among them. Mac often thought that no one liked him. I still remember a good friend of his, Charlotte. He kept a note from her that she passed him in class when he was feeling that everyone was against him. 'They like you more than you think,' it said. Charlotte always tried to cheer him up and they remained good friends. They went on to different secondary schools, but always chatted when they met up in the village or saw each other at village events.

However, Mac did make one very good male friend. His name was Bailey. Bailey was also new to the school and they were kindred spirits in so many ways. This friendship helped Mac in so many ways: they learned that you could fall out and still be friends again – such an important lesson for any child.

The behaviour book

We worked closely with the school to help Mac with any problems. Of course, like many children, he was not often forthcoming about what had happened during the day, so we were not always able to follow issues up if we didn't know about them. We were clear that it was not our job to be his teachers – it was most important to build up our relationship as his parents – but we did want to make sure that we and the school were giving him consistent messages.

It was easy for Mac to gloss over anything difficult that had occurred during the day, especially as he did not want us to know that he had been in trouble.

To begin with, the school's instinct was to try to deal with issues and not to come to us with everything, but we soon realised that what we needed was some form of communication between us so that we could see how things were going, praise Mac for the positives, and help when things weren't going as well as they might. So, the school gave Mac a 'behaviour book' in which they would write about how his day had gone, and we could then follow these reports up with him. It was also a way for us to communicate, as we could let them know if anything difficult was going on at home (for example, he might be getting ready for contact with his brothers) that might affect how he was at school.

The book was a success, until one day it disappeared. We asked where it was, and Mac assured us that his teacher had not written in it. A few weeks later a new one appeared. Then at the end of term, the classrooms were being tidied up, ready to be decorated over the holiday. Swee went to pick up Mac from school and had that familiar feeling as he came out with his teacher and she was beckoned over to the classroom: the sinking feeling that things had gone wrong came back, although Mac's teacher did have a grin on her face. It transpired that during the tidying of the room, Mac's original book had been found in a hatbox that was used for storage in the classroom. He had admitted to hiding it there.

When he got home, I couldn't help but ask him about it. "How did you feel when you put the book in the hatbox, Mac?" I asked.

"Really good, at first," he said. "But then, a bit later, I realised that I would get into trouble, so I didn't feel as good."

I couldn't help but smile. As ever, it was a refreshingly honest answer.

Mac's behaviour did improve and we all got better at reading what he was telling us. About six months after he moved in, I had to go on a work trip to Japan. I had been on short trips before, staying away just for a couple of nights, but this time I was going to be away for a full week – the longest time I had been away from him. I remember as I said goodbye to him, I reassured him that I would talk to him and that I would be back. He just shrugged – he didn't believe me. After all, everyone had left him before.

While I was away, one of Mac's teachers beckoned Swee over when she came to pick him up. Swee wondered what might be wrong now.

"We just wanted to check that everything is OK with your husband away. Mac says that you have been crying every evening. Is there anything that anyone can do to help?"

Swee looked at her in a rather puzzled manner, and then realised what was happening. Mac had a habit of putting his own behaviours onto other people. Actually, Swee had been fine without me (of course!), but Mac had been crying and missing me. His way of telling the teachers was to transfer those emotions to Swee.

When I did get home, I remember how excited Mac was. Part of it was because he realised he was going to get nice, exotic presents, but I think he also realised that I had kept my word and had come back as I'd said I would. The date was particularly significant: the evening I landed back in Britain was the day that Mac's official adoption went through. We would go to court later in June for an official ceremony, but on 14 May 2009, Mac's adoption order went through. When I'd left for Japan he was still in the care of the state, but when I returned I was legally his father and he was legally Macaully Richard George Sutcliffe.

School trips

Mac was lucky to go on a couple of school trips with primary school. For some children this is quite a young age to be away from their parents, but we knew that this was not going to be difficult for Mac as he was used to going to new places and settling in. He also relished the idea of spending all day and his evenings with other children – I think it made him feel a bit like he did when he was living with his brothers.

However, there were still some parents who were uncomfortable about Mac. As I said earlier, we did not share his story with people – it was his private business and up to him when, and if, he decided to share information about his earlier life. One of the downsides of a village is that it is very easy for a vacuum to be filled with misinformation, and to some extent this is what happened. As we had not shared information about whether Mac had been abused, or why he had been taken away from his family, it was easy for rumours to abound, and for that to affect how some saw him. Again, the school were fantastic. They made it clear that there was no good reason why Mac should not be allowed to go, and that if any parents were uncomfortable then they didn't have to send their own children.

Actually, the trip went extremely well for Mac. It was a significant turning point in his school life. He had a great time, but he was also a real comfort to the children who were away from home for the first time and missing their parents. He had real empathy with those who were in pain, and was able to play a 'big brother' role. We noticed a change in him when he came back, and it had certainly helped with his place in the group.

Mac did love to go on all sorts of school trips – I think he enjoyed being out of the school environment, and thrived much more. He also tended to be good with younger children – this was something we saw again and again. He was always very caring, but he particularly loved to be in the older brother role with younger children – as if he was looking for an opportunity to fill that gap that had opened up in his life when he was taken away from his little brother.

School performances

At the end of the first term, the school puts on a Christmas carol service in our local church. I can still remember Mac's first carol service. He was so fidgety that he was positioned next to one of the teaching assistants to make sure he would stand still. If you had been asked to look for the child who stood out (for the wrong reasons!), you would have immediately pointed Mac out. In my experience with Mac, and with other children I have known, it is common for children who have been in care to find it difficult to concentrate, or for them to look around at their surroundings because they are less able to concentrate.

But as Mac moved on through the school, you could see this behaviour start to change, slowly but surely. With each performance, he started to look more and more comfortable. At the end of the summer term, the older years would put on a school play. The younger children would be in the chorus, with the speaking parts taken by the year six children – their starring roles before they moved on to secondary school. However, in year five Mac was asked by the year six teacher if he would like to have a named role in the end-of-year production of *Robin Hood*. They needed an extra boy and, as he was the oldest in year five, they wanted him to have the chance to play Will Scarlet. He was so proud! He got to be the only year five with a named part, and was able to have rehearsals with those who were, in age terms, his peers. I can still remember the feeling, sitting in that hot school hall, watching him as he proudly took to the stage with all of the year six children. It was at that stage that I fully understood the transformation that had taken place over those years. Mac no longer stood out for the wrong reasons. He was able to stand side by side with his peers and others.

In his final year – 2012 – the school put on a special play marking Olympic year (London was hosting the Olympics that year). He was so funny. At last he was one of the gang. On the last day of term, one of the other children had a party at his house for all of his class. Mac had an amazing time. I remember as I picked him up and drove him home, he burst into tears!

"I didn't realise how much I loved that school and how much I'm going to miss it all!"

The transformation was complete. He was still behind his peers in reading and writing, but had made impressive improvements in his social interactions with them – he was as ready as he was ever going to be for the transition to secondary school.

At his leaving assembly, all of the children were given a prize for something that marked out their time at the school. Mac was given an award for 'finding his writer's voice'. Although his spelling was appalling, and never improved, he always loved to write. It helped him to express his feelings and to set out his imagination. From the first notes that he wrote to us and left on our pillow, to poems, songs and stories he used to write in the books that were littered around his very untidy bedroom. His teacher saw that in him even then.

When I was looking through some of Mac's things, I found some of his stories and scribblings – he filled loads of notebooks with songs and stories and phrases, and also like to type things on the family PC. One of them was obviously inspired by the story of the hatbox I mentioned earlier, and I include it here as an example of the things Mac liked to write, exactly as I found it on our family PC (together with his original spellings!).

Tony and the mischievous hatbox!

10.25, lesson two. Tony, as usual, was sat at the very back of the class. The plain, charming face of a lonly boy that is miserable and relentlessly being picked on by his teacher (Mrs Starling). One look of her thieving eyes could turn you to stone. And she knew it…

Tony Henderson has always struggold at school. Being the middel of seven children he was frequently ignored at home.

Mrs Starling had been his year four teacher since September. Although dainty she was a repulsive, cold hearted and savage woman. Her wizened face was framed with wiry hair.

"Tony," she shrieked, "I'm putting you on a behaviour report as you seem to be day-dreaming again!" Tony's eyes began to fill with hot tears, and he could feel the cold stares from the other children. It would be another lonely lunchtime for Tony.

One week into the behaviour report and Tony had had enough. Late at night Tony was laying awake crying trying to think of a plan to hide the report. In the soothing quiet and calm pitch black of his bedroom he came up with a plan. He would hide it in the glove and hat box. It was Autumn. He figured it would be safely away from the prying eyes of Mrs Starling as the sun was still shining and the report could remain undiscovered.

Autumn ended with an icy blast. Mrs Starling leaned over the hat and glove box, and a shiver went down Tony's spine. He had felt overjoyed when he first hid the report, but now felt apprehensive as she opened the lid and stared into its dull depths.

Sadly, it didn't take her long to find the report. She turned her attention to Tony like a Staffordshire Bull Terrier. Tony froze. "Henderson, get here now!" Gingerly he crept towards the snarling teacher. As he walked the whole classed terned and looked at him, his heart sank. He knew his time was up…

With out warning Mrs Starling grabbed the back of his hair, dragging him across the ground towards the front. The other children were petrified. Tony thought he could even hear a few muffled cries from some of the children.

Suddenly Mrs Triffard, the head teacher, burst into room. "Mrs Starling! What on earth is going on!" shrieked Mrs Triffard. It took over ten minutes and two other members of staff to remove Mrs Starling from Tony. The police were called and marched her off the site.

Mrs Triffard invited him into the staff room and made Tony a cup of tea and gave him a biscuit. It was the first time anyone at school had really noticed him. It felt good. His parents come in and took him home early. They were told that Mrs Starling would never be allowed to set foot in the school again. From now on, Tony's school days could only get better and better…

Chapter 7

Contact

Adoption today is very different to the way it was many years ago. My mother, born in 1936, was adopted. It was a very familiar story: her birth mother got 'into the family way' before she was married, when she was seventeen. She was sent away to relatives to have the baby, who was then taken away from her at just a few weeks old. Mum was adopted by my wonderful gran and grandad, who had not been lucky enough to have children of their own. It was organised by their family doctor, as was often the case. My grandparents did not keep this a secret, and told my mum that she was adopted when she was twelve.

Many years later, after my gran had died, we managed to track down and contact Mum's birth family and we now have a close relationship with them all, and have gained a wonderful extended family. As was then the practice, Mum did not have a birth certificate, only her adoption certificate. When she finally decided to track her birth family down, she had to undergo counselling from specialist social workers before she was allowed access to her original birth certificate. From this we were lucky enough to track the family down in the United States, and we were also lucky that everything was so amicable. Although Mum never met her birth mother, who had died some years before, she formed a great relationship with her American half-brothers and -sister and their families. They are now an important part of our family.

For many others the story is quite different. Sometimes they have never been told that they are adopted, and either never find out or find out very late in life. Sometimes birth parents do not want to be reminded of such a painful point in their lives; often feeling so guilty that they did not or could not keep their child. Sometimes it is a painful secret that was never told. My mother was one of the lucky ones. But the point is that there was a complete break with the birth family at the point of adoption.

There are far fewer babies put up for adoption than there were in the past. Children tend to be older and, as such, are likely to have memories of their birth family. They often have siblings or half-siblings who are in different homes, either with family members, in foster care, or in other adoptive families. The situation is much more complicated. Even children who were taken away when very young will know that they are adopted and that they have a birth family, and will have a copy of their birth certificate. They are also likely to have a 'Life Story Book' that will give them information about their birth family – all of this is there to help them come to understand their background and where they have come from. They are given 'ownership' of their own story; something that they can choose in later life to be open about, or to keep as a part of themselves shared only with those they are closest to.

It is made very clear to adoptive parents that they are likely to have to maintain contact with the birth family in some way. It is part of the agreement that is made when the adoption is being applied for. When the child is in foster care, there tends to be more frequent contact with the birth family, and the bond is maintained as there is not the same level of permanence that comes with an adoption.

If a child is placed for adoption, at some point the adoption will be finalised by an adoption order from the family courts. This is applied for by the adoptive parents with the agreement of the adoption authority. Sometimes the birth parents give their consent, but this is not necessary for the adoption order to be granted. The court will decide what is in the best interests of the child. Once the order is made, the adoptive parents are the legal parents with full parental responsibility, and the birth parents lose the legal rights that they had. With this tends to come increased separation, which is important for a successful adoption, to help the child become properly attached to their new parents and family.

I think it's fair to say that contact is still a difficult issue for many adoptive parents; particularly those who have adopted older children. During our training we looked at the issues related to contact a great deal. I could see how important it would be to any child we adopted – although I have to say that explaining that to our family and friends was often more difficult. They found it hard to understand how contact could be beneficial, and would often say that they thought it might confuse the child. I think that is a common and understandable position. In fact, when pushed, some social workers held the same view, even if it wasn't the officially accepted position. And of course, it is always important to consider each individual case on its own merits.

From my experience with Mac, the hard truth about contact is that it is all purely theoretical until you have a new child in your home and you begin to understand the family dynamics from which they have come. With that situation, especially as you are also busily adjusting yourself to this wonderful and challenging new role, as you are falling in love with this child and getting to know them better and better, the issues and emotions around contact can become very complicated indeed.

For many adoptions, contact is fairly straightforward. It might just consist of 'letter-box' contact: probably an annual exchange of letters and photos with birth parents. It's an opportunity for the birth parents and the child to get updates on each other. This is all done through social services to maintain anonymity and to keep addresses and other contact details private. These letters are valuable for the child as it is important that they know that their parents are well, and get up-to-date photos. It helps them understand that time passes, and enables them to prepare for when they reach adulthood and will be able to decide for themselves whether they want to have direct contact. It also helps them realise that their birth parents are growing older, as it can be difficult for them to understand how the passage of time might be affecting them.

Contact arrangements for Mac were more complicated than most. He was one of four brothers, all sharing a birth mother. Mac and his younger brother were full brothers and had always lived together – their relationship was very important to Mac. He tended to worry about his little brother as he had taken a caring role for him in the past, so knowing that he was happy and well was really important. So Mac saw his little brother frequently: initially monthly, and then during school holidays; approximately every six weeks or so. They used to get together for a couple of hours or so at a soft play area and were able to go off and throw themselves around until they were tired.

The first time we met Mac's younger brother and his adoptive parents was at one of the annual sessions when Mac got together with all of his brothers. His older brothers were a fair bit older than him and were half-siblings. It had been decided that it was important that the four brothers did maintain contact annually. To be honest, it was always difficult to decide what to do to keep both the older and the younger boys entertained. What would they all be interested in doing?

The sessions were facilitated by social services. Mac's older brothers both had different fathers to Mac and his younger brother, and had been moved to live with members of their paternal families. None of Mac's brothers were living with their birth mother, but as the older boys were not adopted, they still had plenty of contact with her. Mac's birth parents had not consented to the younger boys' adoptions, so it was important that the older boys should not have direct access to the younger boys' addresses and contact details in case these were then shared with the wider birth family. All contact was intermediated by social workers who specialised in these types of contact, and who had known all of the boys for a number of years.

The first time we all met, Mac had been with us for a couple of months. We were all to meet at a bowling alley that was near to where the older boys lived, as it was more likely that they would come along. We were particularly nervous, as it was the first time that we would meet not only Mac's brothers, but also Mac's younger brother's adoptive parents – the couple who had adopted the younger brother, but not Mac. We were obviously worried about how Mac might react to seeing them, but also not sure how we ourselves would feel when we met them. After all, we had already fallen in love with Mac – it was difficult to understand why it had not worked for them. So, you can imagine that we all approached the contact with some trepidation. Mac was always concerned about meetings whenever social workers were involved. But for his sake we knew we needed to go through with this.

As it happens, meeting his brother's adoptive parents was fine. Of course, it was as awkward for them as it was for us, but I think they took some comfort in seeing that Mac was already settling and appeared to be happy. We spent time with them as the boys went bowling, and got to know them. They had information about Mac's past that they were able to share with us, and we were always happy to pick up as much information as possible, as it was by piecing all sorts of information together that we were able to help Mac manage his feelings about all sorts of situations by starting to understand his past. The contact went well, and after an hour or so we all went our separate ways.

This was the first of our planned annual contact sessions with all of the brothers – and it turned out to be particularly special as it was one of only two occasions when all four brothers made it. One was less reliable in turning up to contact, and it used to upset Mac – after all, he only got the chance to see him once a year. A year is a long time in a ten-year-old boy's life, and if his brother didn't turn up, he knew it would be yet another year until he might see him again. This was particularly hard as he had a very close relationship with him, as his second older brother had looked after him when his parents were not around. It was frustrating for those of us who did make the effort, and no one was able to tell us why he wasn't able to come – in hindsight, we should have realised. One year he did send a note to apologise as he had gone on holiday. Of course, we soon worked out that the holiday was 'at Her Majesty's pleasure'.

This prevented him from coming to an arranged contact meeting a number of times. Luckily Mac's oldest brother always made it, often encouraged by his grandma, and we were able to form a good relationship with both the older brother and the grandma. I have to say, I could never understand why social workers were not able to share the real situation with us, although the more I saw of the system, the more I realised that nothing was joined up, and that communications between different agencies were often very poor.

The contact with Mac's younger brother was more straightforward. Social services were happy to leave the arrangements to us, so we would contact his brother's parents and arrange meetings for half-terms and other school holidays. Mac did find this useful, and although he sometimes wasn't sure how to play with his younger brother (at that age, the gap of two years, coupled with not living together, seemed so big at times), he was always able to see that he was well and getting on OK.

In addition to the face-to-face contact, Mac also had letter-box contact with his birth parents. Once a year, normally around August, we would send a letter with a number of photos and some updates on how Mac was doing – how he was getting on at school, new hobbies, if he'd grown – and in return he would receive a letter back to update him on their news. Well, this was the theory. And we did religiously send the update letter. We would note the things that had happened, collect some photos, and get Mac to write something or draw a picture. Sadly, he only ever received one very short letter back, in the first year. And this is where contact can be very painful.

Mac would look forward to all sorts of contact. In fact, we began to notice that in the week running up to a contact meeting his behaviour would get worse. He would be distracted, he would behave worse at school, he became more withdrawn and rude. At the beginning this was particularly the case when social workers were involved. Mac's past experience of meetings with social workers was that they often led to him being moved on to a new home – and it was a while before he was confident enough to know that any meeting with a social worker would not now mean that he was going to be leaving us. Once the adoption order went through, he finally began to believe that this was going to be for the long term.

But Mac was also nervous before contact because he was never sure how things would work out and if all of his brothers would turn up. The meeting was really important to him, but he also knew that he was quite likely to be disappointed, and he didn't know who to blame. Coming back from contact was often a sad car journey – sometimes quiet, but as time moved on and Mac began to trust us even more, he would open up about how he felt, and about how he felt let down. It was for all of these reasons that we decided to ensure that contact was held during school holidays – at least then it interfered less with his schoolwork.

But Mac was most disappointed by the fact that he did not receive letters from his birth parents. Once we had sent our letter, he would wait patiently for the post every morning, longing for some sort of letter or photo. But except in that first year, no letter came. It was another example of Mac being let down, and it was always difficult for him. Over time, it became less of an issue, and we tended to ensure that we had exciting summer holidays as a distraction so that he could concentrate on that and not sit waiting for a letter that never came. In the end, Swee and I always kept our part of the agreement by sending a letter and a photo to his birth mother. But we didn't make much of it with Mac. It was a letter from us, his parents, to his birth mother, so that she would be able to see that all was well and that he was happy.

Modern contact issues

When we adopted Mac, social media was non-existent. It was not the case that everyone had a smartphone and thus constant contact with all sorts of people. It was just not something to think about. But as Mac grew up and approached secondary school, it became an expectation for most children that they would get a mobile phone – and Mac was no different.

So, when he turned twelve, just before he started at secondary school, he got his first phone. As he got older, he wanted (needed, in his mind!) more and more powerful phones as social media began to take off. And, being indulgent parents, we normally acceded to his requests (although he did tend to get my cast-offs when I upgraded).

Being responsible parents, we tried our best to keep up with the technology so that we could understand what Mac was able to do online, and I would sit down with him as we gave him greater access to things and ensure that we all understood if he was safe or not. Of course, this is something that all parents have to be aware of these days – the internet can be a dangerous place. But for parents of adopted children, it can also be a place for their child to start trying to contact their birth family, and for the birth family to find ways of contacting the child.

For our own part, we were fairly sure that this would happen at some point. Although all contact issues are tricky at times, for Mac they were particularly complicated. With three brothers, two of whom were still in regular contact with their birth family, it was inevitable that Mac would be able to track down members of his birth family very easily. What we were most keen on was that Mac should be honest with us and not keep any of this a secret. We also didn't want him to feel guilty. Eventually he did get access to his birth family – unknown to us, his brothers had shared their phone numbers with him in a contact session and everything grew from there. Once Mac was on Facebook, the cat was out of the bag. Of course, we could have insisted that he keep everything private, but we were keen that there should be no conflict around all of this, and the more we knew then, the more we would be able to travel the path with Mac and not be excluded from this part of his life. It seems to me that modern social media makes it next to impossible to avoid birth family being able to make contact with your adopted child, unless your child has no interest and does not want to be found. It is an issue that you have to think carefully about and be prepared for.

Mac and I would have quite open conversations about his phone calls with his birth family. He did not tell them where he lived – it was still important for him to be able to keep that part of his life safe and protected. But he did talk to them from time to time; mostly just his birth mother and his two older brothers, and sometimes his birth father too. He would normally tell me about these chats afterwards. I would always make sure that I showed no negative reaction to ensure he didn't clam up in the future (though of course, part of me was always worried about what could happen as a result of this contact). What it did for Mac was enable him to establish a relationship of sorts with his birth parents, so that when he was old enough to decide if he wanted to see them again, he would be better informed. And it filled the gap that was left by the lack of letters.

However difficult contact issues are for the parents involved, it is small fry compared to the conflicting loyalties that the child is feeling. It was very interesting to me that Mac would never phone his birth family from our house. He would go out on his bike for a ride around the village and call them while he was out. I told him it was OK to speak to them from home, and that his room was soundproofed enough that we wouldn't be able to hear the conversation, but I think he wanted there to be a physical separation between his home and his birth family. In his mind, the safety of his home was very much tied up with us and separate from his birth family. This behaviour never changed.

In the end, though, I think Mac was able to balance his loyalties, and that was so important for his well-being. He knew that we were his parents, and that we would always stand by him, keep him safe, and let him have whatever he needed. But you should never underestimate the 'pull' of birth parents, especially on a child adopted at an older age.

One post on Facebook made me happy that Mac had sorted these things in his own mind. On Father's Day 2016, he posted, 'Happy Father's Day, to both my dads.' I think this said it all – and thanks to autocorrect, he even got the spelling right!

Chapter 8

Special Occasions

I think it's pretty common, if you are longing for children, to spend some time imagining special occasions and how they might be when you do have children. Birthday parties, Christmas, and family occasions more generally are all very different as a parent of a young child. I know that once we had been approved for adoption, I often thought about and planned what Christmas would be like, and what I would want to do to make things special when a child finally moved into our home and became part of our family – but then I have always been an inveterate planner. The thing to be aware of is that the adopted child has been doing the same thing: dreaming of how they wish things could be, and how they hope things will be once they have a family of their own.

Once we had adopted Mac, we looked forward to these occasions and the opportunity to 'show him off' to our family and friends, knowing that they were going to love him as much as we already did. We were so keen for him to be surrounded by the family that we cared about so much, and to be enveloped in their love. We had been warned, to begin with, to introduce people slowly as moving into a new home is a pretty daunting prospect – it is most important that the attachment between parents and child begins to build, giving the child some much-needed stability and an opportunity to build trust. We were careful to follow this advice. We introduced Mac slowly to the closest members of our family – his new grandparents, aunts and uncles, and cousins – and he lapped it up, glad to be the centre of attention and revelling in the treats that they all inevitably had for him.

So, we felt he was ready for the first family party – which was to be a gathering of much of our family for a Chinese meal to celebrate my father's seventy-fifth birthday, in the third week of December, just about a month after Mac had moved in. The family had hired a private room upstairs in the restaurant, so it was the perfect opportunity, with no one else around.

The first error we made was timing. Swee and I are always early for everything, as is the rest of our family. Our intention had been to get to the restaurant early enough to make sure that we could get a comfortable place to sit, and one where Mac would like to be sitting next to his choice of family member. Of course, as trainee parents we didn't factor in the extra time needed to get out of the door when you have an eight-year-old in tow. So, not surprisingly, we arrived last.

The room was a little on the tight side for the number of people, and Mac was desperate to sit next to Grandy (as my dad was known), but that was not possible. And although it was just six days before Christmas, and fairly cold outside, it was extremely hot in the room already. Things quickly deteriorated. Mac was getting in a worse and worse mood, getting hotter and hotter and not doing anything that he was told to do. We wanted to enjoy the evening and we had built it up to be a fun night, but the truth was that it was just too overwhelming for him. So, the only thing to do was to leave – with me literally carrying an eight-year-old Mac under my arm, crying and quite upset and very hot. Classic parenting fail.

Actually, as soon as we left the restaurant and got into the car, everything calmed down, so we got pizza and went home. What we also didn't know was that Mac was starting to come down with a nasty cold and a temperature – probably a reaction to all the changes he had been through in the last few months.

It is interesting that we found that an almost sure-fire way to get Mac to calm down in any situation was to take him over a threshold. It was more than just taking him out of the situation: we found that if you got him through a door, it would often take the heat out of the situation. This was most useful in the mornings. Mac always woke up happy, and was usually fairly content to go to school. However, in the early days, when he first started testing the boundaries, we did find him starting to kick up at going-to-school time. We were always very clear that school was non-negotiable. Even if he was very upset in the house, if I managed to get him out of the front door, he calmed down almost immediately. (I have since read somewhere that there is scientific research that shows that humans' emotional states do change when they cross a threshold – so maybe there is something in it.)

Christmas

Of all of the special occasions that I had thought most about, Christmas must come top of the list. It is commonly said that Christmas is for children, and it has to be true that the Christmas traditions are so much more exciting when you're a child or when you are the parent of younger children. When my nephews were younger, I would always spend Christmas Eve at my sister's house, so that I could join in the preparations for Christmas morning and be there when my nephews woke up to see what Father Christmas had left and to open their presents.

I have always loved the run-up to Christmas as well. I love all of those schmaltzy Christmas films, and the nights drawing in. I love the preparing of Christmas treats – making the pudding and the cake weeks in advance, with those familiar, warm Christmas spices scenting the air. Then come the carol concerts and midnight Mass, by candlelight in our beautiful village church. Swee always loved Christmas – decorating the house, shopping for the perfect presents, wrapping them beautifully. And of course, Christmas carols piped around the house at every opportunity.

So you can imagine how excited we were for Mac's first Christmas. We had already taken him to Lapland UK, and encouraged him to write his Christmas letter to Father Christmas. Our preparations were under way. Well, they had been under way in our heads for years, and we had started to buy presents as soon as we knew for sure that Mac would be moving in. We'd thought carefully about what traditions we wanted to start with him and how things might work.

The run-up to Christmas was fun. My birthday is the same day as my dad's, just a few days before Christmas. As Dad's dinner had been a big affair with which Mac had not coped well, we kept mine quiet and limited to the three of us when my actual birthday came around. Mac loved to buy presents for people, so Swee and he had been shopping for me. We also had a delicious Dalek cake. Mac was right in the middle of his fluey bug, and so was feeling pretty under the weather, but the cake and the birthday tea helped to raise his spirits.

As Christmas drew nearer, we started to talk about Father Christmas more. I loved to stop still, really quietly, and say, "Can you hear those sleigh bells? Listen carefully. Father Christmas's getting ready to come." Mac would stop and listen, a look of wonder on his face, and finally would convince himself that he could hear them.

We were careful not to do too much of the good boy/bad boy stuff. Adopted children have such low self-esteem that you do not want to make them feel bad about themselves. (As a digression, years later, when Mac had moved on from the Father Christmas myth, I asked him what things had been like before he moved to Sue and Mark's, which was where he'd had his first real Christmas. He said, "Father Christmas never came. I just assumed I hadn't been good enough to get any presents, and that he would never want to come and visit me." I think it was one of the saddest things he ever said.)

Swee and Mac had spent ages decorating the house and the tree. It became their 'thing', something they always did together, having a similar taste for all things spangly and fairy lights! Finally we got to Christmas Eve. Mac got some sherry, a mince pie, and a carrot for Rudolph, put it all on a special Christmas plate and placed it on the top of the wood burner. I always cooked the turkey on Christmas Eve, and a ham. I still have a picture of Mac looking at that bronzed turkey, which looks huge against him – he has a look of disbelief at the size of it. He also found that he loved Christmas ham – it became one of his absolute favourites. We spent the day watching Father Christmas's journey on the PC via the North American Aerospace Defense Command (NORAD) website – it was so good to see him making progress around the world. We sat down and watched some telly; then there was one last check on NORAD and Mac went to bed. We read *The Night Before Christmas* together and he went off to sleep. Then it was all systems go as Swee and I got his presents together in the various sacks that we had – one of which we had made with his name on. We couldn't believe the number of presents we had for him. It is true that we may have gone overboard.

I went off to midnight Mass. When I came back, we put Mac's presents on the sofa in the sitting room, by the tree. We also had some instant snow, and so made footprints with it leading to his presents from the patio door. The last thing to do was to hang up a stocking in his bedroom with a few small surprises. I had never had to do anything like that before. I crept into Mac's room every night to kiss him goodnight when I went to bed and he never woke up, but the stakes this night were so high – I didn't want him to wake and for it all to be ruined. Of course, Mac had made things more difficult by falling asleep facing his door! Anyway, he had a chest of drawers by the door, and I was able to quietly slip the stocking over the handle and creep out without waking him up.

In fact he slept really well that night. The next morning, he woke up about six and came in to see us. We had made sure that there were enough things in his stocking to keep him occupied, at least for a little while. He brought it through to our bedroom.

"Father Christmas's been!" he said, with utter delight on his face.

"Let's go and see if he has left anything downstairs," I replied.

So he led us downstairs. (I had that groggy feeling, having been to bed late following the late church service.) The door to the sitting room was closed. Mac opened it, and as he went into the room his face lit up. He couldn't decide what to do first.

He went to the fire. "Look – the drink has gone, and the mince pie. And Rudolph has eaten half of the carrot. It must be him – I can see the teeth marks!"

Swee had done a perfect job with the carrot – he was completely convinced.

He went to the footprints and felt the 'snow'. "It's still cold!" he said. (It actually wasn't; just wet.)

He then went to start opening his presents. The thing I remember most is that he took his time. He savoured and enjoyed opening each one. It took ages, and he enjoyed every minute of it. As always, he also loved giving presents to me and Swee – his generosity shining through.

The rest of the day went equally well. The family always spends Christmas at my sister's house just five minutes away, with her family, Swee's mum, dad and brother, and my mum and dad. My nephew has a daughter just a year or so younger than Mac, so they were able to sit together and have a good time chatting away.

All in all, it was a perfect Christmas. Looking back, it could have been so overwhelming. But starting with just the three of us and then being with the family worked (and by then, Mac knew all of the family). The other thing we learned very quickly was that sometimes when a lot of us were together, Mac needed to go off on his own for some peace and quiet. He would disappear for a little while and then come back when he was ready. It's easy to forget that he was often dealing with some conflicting emotions: wondering what people from his past were up to, and maybe even feeling guilty that he was having a better time than them. Those are difficult emotions for an eight-year-old to process.

We had four Christmases with Mac still believing in all the magic – although it has to be said that the last one involved a bit of brinkmanship as to who was going to crack first. I'm sure Mac felt that if he stopped believing, the presents might stop coming. He never asked for too much, and we did always try to get some sort of surprise for him. Even when he was fifteen he was grateful. I remember that I finally got him his own iPad – he had no idea.

When he opened the parcel, he looked amazed. "Is this for me?"

Those Christmases are still some of my best memories.

Mother's Day

Mother's Day is so painful for many people at some time in their lives – if they have lost their mother, if they have lost a child, if they are childless – and once Swee and I were married and trying unsuccessfully for a baby, Mother's Day was very difficult.

Once we had Mac, we started to look forward to Mother's Day in a completely different way. It was going to be a celebration of the fact that we had finally become a family. And for us that meant going to church, as we had so much to be thankful for.

Our church, like so many, gives out flowers to mothers on Mothering Sunday. But the children often also make gifts for their mothers. I can still remember sitting with Swee in the pew as Mac went up to the front to help give out the presents. The children had made little pretend 'handbags' from face flannels, containing soap and other smellies. They were in different colours, but Mac knew that Swee loved all shades of blue, and looked carefully for a blue one. He rushed back to her with the biggest smile on his face as he launched himself at her to give her the present and a huge hug. I felt so emotional and happy, and I can't imagine how Swee felt.

As it was Swee's first Mother's Day, the rest of the family came back to our house for lunch. It was a typical get-together and we had had a few since Mac had been with us, so we thought nothing of it. But fairly soon after lunch started, Mac became really quiet and pensive. Then he went off to his room on his own.

You see, through all the excitement, including Mac's own, we hadn't thought enough about the conflicting emotions that he was feeling. Here, for the first time, he was celebrating Mother's Day with a woman who wasn't the first he'd called 'Mum'. Even though in many people's eyes his birth mother had let him down and not played the role of a mother, she was still his mum and still very important to him. Despite the fact that he was angry and upset with her for so many occasions when she hadn't been there for him, he still loved her.

And here I have to say that it takes a while as an adoptive parent to come to terms with that. However understanding you try to be, you know that your child's birth parents have let down and hurt the child who is now yours, whom you love as much as you would your own biological child, and it is difficult to forgive them. We always made sure that we never let these feelings show in front of Mac, and over the years, as you realise how important the birth parents still are to your child, the angry feelings subside.

That first Mother's Day, we had forgotten the huge conflict of emotions that Mac would have, and didn't make sufficient allowances for them. But we did learn a lesson. From then on, at any other big family occasion, we would make an effort to mention Mac's birth family so that he knew they were not forgotten and to make sure he realised it was OK to be thinking about them. It was always a tricky line to tread, because as Mac grew older he made it clear that they were *his* family, not ours. But we would still mention them as I think it was important as he grew to give him permission to think about them and to know that it didn't hurt us. We knew he loved us and loved his home and all that it stood for – but there was still room for him to think about and love his birth family.

Chapter 9

First Holidays

Cornwall

Mac didn't have a passport when he first came to us, and we weren't able to apply for one until the adoption order was granted some six months after he moved in. But we were keen to go away as a family to spend some time together in different, more relaxed surroundings. We decided to find a cottage to rent, and found a nice complex in Cornwall. It had a pool, was near the beach, and wasn't far from the Eden Project, and so had plenty to occupy us for a week. It also had a nice, secure garden, so we could take the dogs with us.

So, we set off on the drive down. It was the longest car journey we had been on with Mac and the dogs, so we weren't quite sure how it would go. But we shouldn't have worried: the dogs and Mac slept all of the way.

It was such a lovely place to go away together. Being in a cottage meant that we were free to do whatever we wanted. We also took loads of DVDs to watch if the weather wasn't bad (it was the February half-term!). But we ended up spending most of our time in the wonderful, heated indoor pool. Although the pool was shared by about ten cottages in the complex, it was often quiet. We also found that most of the families would get up early for the day and then the place was empty and we had everything to ourselves.

To be honest, Mac most enjoyed being in the pool in any case. It was on that holiday that he became a real water baby. Swee loved swimming and was a very strong swimmer, it being one of her major hobbies when she was young. When Mac came to us he was not able to swim. He loved the water, but had never had the opportunity to learn. In just a week, by visiting the pool every day, he started swimming. He got very good by the end of the week: it was clear that he was a natural in the water.

We did have one trip out to the Eden Project, and we all loved walking through the biodomes, seeing the extraordinary range of different plants. And it was somewhere warm to go on a chilly day. Most of the rest of the holiday we just relaxed, swam, went out for pub lunches, played with the dogs, and watched fun DVDs. It was such a good holiday and a good chance for all of us to have a rest after our first months together.

We returned to that complex a couple more times – it was perfect in so many ways. One year, Mac and I went with my mum and dad as Swee had just come out of hospital after recovering from a nasty infection. It was during the summer, so we were able to do more things. We found the beach – a fantastic and remote sandy beach. When we first visited, the sea was a long way out and it was an incredibly long walk to get anywhere near. We collected shells and pebbles, and Mac dug the deepest holes. We have a picture of him in a hole that he just kept digging. And again we went and swam every day in the pool – sometimes twice a day.

Our last visit was less successful. We weren't able to book our usual cottage, so weren't able to take the dogs. That was OK, as they were always happy to go to our local kennels. They were pretty old by then so wouldn't have enjoyed the journey and didn't do much more than sleep in any case. Swee had been feeling sick, but we decided to set off anyway. We should have known to turn back when she started being physically ill. It became our longest journey to Cornwall as we stopped every half-hour or so for her to throw up. Looking back, I can't imagine why we kept going! I think Mac was so excited to be going and to be able to swim every day that we didn't want to disappoint him. When we got to the cottage, Swee opted to go straight to bed. Overnight she got much sicker, and started running a temperature. We called a doctor and he agreed to prescribe her some anti-sickness tablets. Mac and I then had to find the surgery and a local chemist. This shouldn't have been too difficult, except it decided to rain – and not just rain. It was so torrential that there were rivers of water running down the narrow Cornish roads. We couldn't see a thing. Somehow we managed to track down the GP and get Swee her medicine. After a day, she started to feel better and we all managed to enjoy the rest of the holiday – more swimming, more pub lunches, and more digging at the beach. Perfect family holidays.

Cottage holidays worked well when we wanted a short half-term break – as long as there was a pool. We visited a few more cottages over the years as a family, often also taking Mum and Dad or Swee's brother, Andy. Andy came with us to the best cottage we visited. It had been built as an extension to the owner's property in Cornwall, and it had its own garden and surroundings. But the best feature was the private indoor swimming pool. Andy is as much a water baby as Swee and Mac. He and Mac spent hours swimming and splashing around in the pool. It was another great family break.

For me the most important thing about holidays is the memories, and I can honestly say that some of our best memories date from those holidays – halcyon days.

Euro Disney

I had never been to Euro Disney. Swee had been when she was much younger and had always wanted to go back when we had children. So, once the adoption order was granted, we applied for Mac's passport and booked up to go. We planned to go in the October half-term of 2009, just before our one-year anniversary of Mac moving in. We were going for a long weekend which took in Halloween. We decided to push out the boat and go for everything: we booked first-class tickets on the Disney Eurostar and got tickets for the special Halloween party in the park on Halloween evening after the park had closed.

This was the first time that Mac had been abroad, so he was very excited. Rather than us taking the train up to St Pancras, my dad agreed to drive us up. We arrived nice and early and settled in to wait for the train. The station was full of excitement as there were so many people there, ready to board the *Disney Express*. There were barbershop quartets and bands to entertain us. In no time, it was time to take our seats. In first class, we had loads of space. We relaxed and got ready to enjoy the journey.

Mac's eyes were wide with excitement. He enjoyed it as we moved through the Kent countryside, and then soon enough we were going through the Channel Tunnel. He was a little nervous, I think, until we came out. As we watched the French countryside speed by (as the train was then allowed to go at full speed), we pointed out the differences in the landscape. Simple things like electricity pylons looked different, and the houses we could see were not the typical Victorian terraces that were beside the railway track on the English side of the Channel.

Our tickets were checked and we were given all sorts of passes that would allow us into the parks and the special parties. Disney characters moved up and down the train, keeping the children (and most of the adults, to be fair) in an excitable state. But there is no doubt that the highlight of the journey for Mac was the breakfast. It was a cooked breakfast, and delicious. There was delicious, dark French coffee for the adults, but for the children there was hot chocolate. But not just any hot chocolate: it was thick and sweet. Mac's eyes lit up as he saw it – he couldn't believe it. He often had hot chocolate at home, but it was nothing like this. He drank it down and had the cutest chocolate moustache.

After a couple of hours or so, we arrived at the Euro Disney site. Our cases were taken away and we were able to visit the park while we were waiting for our rooms to be ready later that afternoon.

We walked into the main park. Now, it is easy to be cynical about all things Disney, but I don't think anything prepares you for that first look as you walk in through the gates and walk down Main Street, looking at the fairy-tale castle ahead. I think you have to be pretty hard-hearted not to be taken in by the Disney magic to some extent. I know I was surprised by how much it moved me. It's fair to say that Disney know how to conjure up the magic.

The first thing we did was go into the first shop on Main Street. We wanted to buy an autograph book so that Mac could get the autographs of the Disney characters. He wasn't really sure what to do at first – we saw Eeyore (my favourite!), and he watched as the other children went up and had their photos taken and got their books signed. He ventured up tentatively with me and asked for an autograph. Eeyore gave him a huge hug, and we took a picture and then had his book signed. Mac soon got the idea as we walked round the park, rushing up and getting hugs and autographs – we were able to put a picture of each hug in his autograph book. It is such a beautiful memento. Mac spent the rest of the holiday looking for new characters and going up to talk to them and get their signatures.

Pretty soon after we had come out of the shop there was an afternoon parade. Disney do these so well. We were in a perfect place to see all of the characters and floats as they turned around at the end of Main Street. We were pointing out all of the characters to Mac, and soon realised that he didn't know who any of them were. He had clearly missed out on watching Disney films when he was young and didn't know many of them, apart from some of the ones we had watched together. Clearly, we needed to work on his Disney education – very easy in a hotel room set up to play back-to-back Disney movies!

It was time to head for our hotel as our room was now ready. We were staying in Hotel New York, just a short walk from the parks. Just outside the hotel was a large hot-air balloon. It was tethered to the ground, but raised up into the air so that you could get an unparalleled view of the parks. Mac was desperate to go in it. It was late afternoon, but still light, and there was no one waiting, so it seemed like the best time. I had forgotten that Swee was terrified of heights – she didn't even like driving down steep hills or going over long bridges – but she agreed. We paid our euros and got in.

It was just us and one other couple. The 'basket' was actually made of metal and was like a large doughnut with a hole in the middle where the winching equipment was housed. You could walk around the ring and see the views from all angles. During the five-minute ride the balloon went up about 100 metres – apparently you can see up to twenty kilometres away. Mac loved it and wanted to walk all around, but then I noticed Swee's face: she looked pale and had a fixed grin. She did not look comfortable. She was holding on to the side of the basket and didn't move – this was awkward as the other couple could not get past us and had to go round the other way! (Swee had once gone on the London Eye with our nephew and spent the whole time sitting on the bench in the middle with her eyes closed.) Luckily, the five minutes were soon over and we were able to make our way to the hotel and get Swee a much-needed cup of coffee.

After we unpacked, we went to find somewhere to eat – it was a rather bizarre German-themed restaurant, but the food was good. We then decided that it had been a long day and there was lots to do in the morning, so went back to our hotel for an early night.

The rest of our time at the resort was fantastic and there is just too much to go into everything in detail, but I thought I'd include a few highlights and some lessons we learned about Mac as we were still only a year in.

First, the lessons: Mac had a couple of meltdowns during the holiday. These were still fairly common and we were beginning to learn that there was a pattern to them, although we were still not confident enough in ourselves to always believe that given time he would come out of the temper. And I think all parents will recognise the embarrassment of a wildly misbehaving nine-year-old, and the fact that in public you don't always have the patience that you might at home. But we were getting better at spotting the signs: they were generally connected to tiredness, or more strictly being overwhelmed, which tended to become more apparent when Mac was tired. When he was getting tired he was definitely less resilient. He still could not deal with too much choice, but wanted to feel that he did have some control over what we chose to do. We were starting to get better at building parameters around those choices for him. The key with Mac was to keep the choices to two options. Anything more was just overwhelming for him. Suddenly he had all of these new experiences being thrown at him, and he didn't know how to deal with everything at once. If he did have a meltdown, we would always try to just move him out of the situation. As I mentioned before, physically crossing a threshold to somewhere new often calmed things down – and we would always use the counting trick that the social workers had taught us. And Swee and I had got better at sensing when things were getting out of control, and were able to sense the change in Mac's mood and avoid a meltdown a little more often.

Now the highlights. Mac loved all sorts of rides and had no fear at all. On the other hand, I am useless with them. Mac was prepared to go on rides on his own as long as we were around, but I felt that I needed to be a good dad and try. One morning we got to Big Thunder Mountain early, before there were any queues. Swee told me she had been on it before and it was fine (she lied!). So we got on and set off. Of course, Big Thunder Mountain is made to look, feel and sound like a ride on a rickety old train. Although I knew that, my mind went into overdrive and I was terrified from beginning to end. I can't tell you how high we got because I kept my eyes closed the whole time! Mac, on the other hand, was cheering and putting his arms up and having a great time. When we got off, I found my wife in hysterics – she said she could hear me from the ground!

After that, Mac went on all the scary rides with us watching. However, we did enjoy some rides together. We enjoyed our time on the *Pirates of the Caribbean* ride. Mac loved the films and was so excited to see Jack Sparrow and all of the other characters. Swee and Mac had loads of turns on the *Toy Story* ride, having a best time shooting all of the aliens. But the big surprise hit was It's a Small World. Once we had gone round on those little boats and listened to the fairly annoying tune, Mac wanted to go on loads more times – it just hit home with the younger child in him.

We also loved the Halloween party. After the park closed on our second night, there was a special party with a lit parade and a fantastic light show at the castle. We were all encouraged to dress up, and Swee had brought witch and wizard costumes for us and a skeleton costume for Mac. It was spectacular – the sort of display that Disney does so well.

One night we went to the Buffalo Bill show. It consisted of cowboys and Native Americans, and amazing horse riding, knife throwing, shooting, and all sorts of other tricks. We were all given a hat when we entered, and the colour of our section indicated the team we were supporting during the competition. It was brilliant – the atmosphere was fantastic and we all spent most of the evening open-mouthed.

The final highlight was the character breakfast. We had booked that for one of the mornings. We went along to the designated restaurant and loads of different characters came to our tables for photos, hugs and autographs.

Mac was by now keen to meet all of the different characters. A particular favourite was Goofy. A little later he confided in me, saying, "I know they're not real, Dad. They're just people in costumes. I could see the join!"

So I replied, "That's true. Except for Mickey: he's real and he's magic!"

Mac gave a huge grin, absolutely convinced that it was true – Mickey Mouse really *is* magic!

Cruises

The other sort of holiday that we always enjoyed was a cruise. We had been on a few cruises before Mac came to us, but thought that we would try one with him to see if he liked it.

We booked a cruise to the Mediterranean. Mac loved it. Modern cruise ships have loads of entertainment on offer for the kids. The kids' clubs are great, and Mac loved to go along and spend time there. It gave him an opportunity to make a few friends. The staff were also perfect: they tended to act in a big brother/big sister way, rather than feign a parental relationship which the kids could get plenty of the rest of the time. It also gave Mac a degree of autonomy which he always valued. We were happy to give him as much freedom as was appropriate and he never abused it…well, except once!

The key card for the cabin also acts as a payment card in the on-board shops. Mac's card was limited so that he couldn't buy things he was not old enough for, but he could buy drinks and ice creams while he was out. We were able to monitor his spending on the account. Mac had always been extremely generous, and he loved to buy presents, especially for Swee. He found that the shop sold sparkly nail varnish, and he bought that for her and excitedly presented it to her – actually, he tended to have good taste and it was perfect for a forthcoming formal evening.

Buoyed by this experience, he did then get a little carried away. He had met some friends in the clubs and they sometimes had some free time during which they could wander around. He had been out for a while and was due back. For some reason I decided to check the balance on our account, which you could do on the cabin's TV screen, and it showed that Mac had spent quite a large sum (approximately £50) in one of the shops. When he came back he was a little sheepish, so I had to ask if there was something he wanted to tell me. Nothing was forthcoming at first – until I showed Mac my little secret: that I could see exactly what he was spending on his card. He went pale and took something out of his pocket.

On sea days, the shops tend to have special promotions to get you to spend as much money as you can. A regular feature is the 'inch of gold', which consists of various different chains on large wheels that are metres long and can be cut to your desired length and turned into bracelets or necklaces. Mac had always been something of a magpie and had succumbed, egged on by one of his friends, to acquire a matching necklace and bracelet in very chunky faux silver curb chain. I could see that he had second thoughts. I was in two minds as to what to do as inside I wanted to laugh out loud, because he had just got carried away and immediately thought better of it. Swee was not helping as she was also on the verge of laughing. On the other hand, I did want Mac to learn the value of money. So, we had a little chat. I promised that he wasn't in trouble, but said I wanted him to understand that he couldn't just go and buy things without asking. I did also point out that the chain was 'tat' and would turn his skin green in no time at all, especially if he went swimming in it. By this point he was feeling a little sorry for himself and said he didn't like it anyway and just wanted to throw it away. We started to laugh gently, not wanting him to think we were laughing at him, and eventually we were all laughing and put it all down to experience. But there was one consequence: we kept the chains and said that if he ever thought of abusing money again, he should just think of the lessons he'd learned with those chains! I still have them to this day.

We went on a number of cruises with Mac and other members of our family. They always made great family holidays. Mac loved the new ports and the visits ashore. He got to go to so many places: a trip round Venice on a small boat, the Barcelona football stadium, the place where port is made in Porto, and many more. We encouraged (and helped) him to keep a journal on the cruises to help him with his reading and writing during the holidays, but also as a lasting memento. He loved dressing up in smart suits with all of the family and sitting down to nice meals. He also went swimming and tried all sorts of other activities, like the FlowRider surfing simulator and the skydiving simulator. They were all perfect family holidays – and he never did buy any more tat!

Chapter 10

Mac and Church

In the information pack that we got about Mac before we met him there was a statement that said, 'Mac doesn't do church.' I thought it was a rather strange comment but didn't think anything more of it.

When we were going through the adoption approval process, I was also going through the selection process to train as a part-time non-stipendiary priest in the Church of England. (A non-stipendiary priest is one who is an unpaid volunteer. We are still normally attached to a parish or group of parishes, and do all of the same things as those priests who are paid.) It was a rather odd time, going through two processes that were particularly probing and intrusive at the same time. We did also find sometimes that social services were suspicious of Christians, feeling for some reason that we would force religion on any child who came to live with us. This was never an issue for us. I had always gone to church with my dad when I was young, but was never forced to. Swee had gone when she was very young, but not when she was a little older. It was very clear to both of us that Mac could come to church if he wanted to – and we wanted him to feel comfortable in church as I would be spending so much time there, but he could certainly stay at home with Swee if he didn't want to.

Once Mac did move in with us, I remember asking him a few questions about Christmas and Easter, and he had clearly learned the basics at school or in one of his foster homes as he knew about the birth of Jesus at Christmas and that Jesus died on Good Friday. Fairly early on, we took him to one of the family services as lots of our friends wanted to meet him. I remember sitting in the pew with him and Swee – he enjoyed looking around at what was going on, and singing along to the hymns he knew. Of course, his reading wasn't good enough to follow the words of the service, although I did try to trace them along with him. And then it came to the Lord's Prayer – and he started reciting it along with everyone else! He knew all of the words. Talking to him later, he said that he'd learned it at school, but had also used to go along to church quite often with his last foster mum, Sue. So, whenever Swee went to church, he tended to go along with her as well. He enjoyed going along to the special services like Mother's Day and the Christingle at Christmas.

When Mac moved in, I had just been approved for training, but I decided I would put it off for a year while he settled in as I knew it would take a lot of my spare time. However, I did still get involved in some services and I was in the church choir.

Early on, I was going to help with evensong, and I had just put my cassock on. Mac hadn't seen me in it before. He was in his bedroom, and as I walked past from our bedroom I shouted goodbye to him. He looked at me and said, "You're not going out like that!"

I couldn't help but laugh. Actually, Mac became quite intrigued, and he decided to join the church choir. He loved to sing and enjoyed being part of the group. I think he also enjoyed having his own red cassock as part of the choir. I did sometimes take services in some of our other churches, but Mac would still go along to our local church to sing in the choir. Dad was one of the churchwardens, so Mac was able to help out: lighting the candles and putting them out after the service (a particular favourite, as he was always a little pyromaniac), handing out books, and helping with the collection and counting it afterwards. It was a good chance for him to have some independence and to spend time with my dad. I think he loved being part of the church community and being comfortable in the church. He also had a chance to earn extra money by singing in the choir at weddings – always a special treat!

Mac's baptism

Once Mac was adopted, we spoke to him and he agreed with us that he would like to be baptised. For us it was a way to give thanks for our family coming together and for Mac to be welcomed by the village and the church family in a formal way. We set a date for September 2009, close to my mum's birthday.

One thing that he was very sure about was that he wanted to have some new clothes, and to be smart. Mac was starting to enjoy having nice clothes and was becoming a bit of a peacock. So, he and I went shopping. We thought a suit might be a bit too much, but found him a waistcoat and a smart shirt. He also saw a vivid neon pink tie that he loved, so that topped the outfit off. Mac also wanted some new shoes. He always found his school shoes boring. As any parent of a boy will know, school shoes take a lot of damage, particularly from plenty of football in the playground during break times. So Mac's shoes were suitably comfortable and hard-wearing.

When we were shopping he saw a pointy pair of shoes that he immediately fell in love with. So we agreed that he could have them, as long as they were just for church and special occasions, and not to be worn to school. (He agreed, although there were one or two occasions when he tried to slip past us with them on for school, claiming that his others were too dirty or uncomfortable.)

We decided that we would make it a great big party and take the opportunity to celebrate with everyone. We needed to choose who we wanted as godparents. There were so many people who were important to us and whom we wanted to be important in Mac's life. We felt he needed lots of godparents – so we chose ten! And where any of those were part of a couple, we stressed that we were actually asking all of the family to support us and him. We had:

- My sister Sandra and her two sons (our nephews), Daniel and Richard.
- Swee's sister Annie and her daughter (our niece), Emily.
- Swee's brother Andy.
- Our friend Adam (and, by association, his wife and children).
- Our friend Jon (and again, his wife and children).
- Our friend Rebecca (and her husband and children).
- Sue, Mac's last and very special foster carer (which naturally included Mark).

Five men and five women. There wasn't much space around the font! The service was lovely and the church was packed with all the people we had invited and plenty of others as well. I was worried that Mac might be a little overwhelmed, but he took it all in his stride.

We had also planned a party afterwards in our local village hall. This was to be a celebration of us coming together as a family, and to thank everyone for all of the support that they had given. We decided to have a *Harry Potter* theme. Each of the tables was named after a *Harry Potter* character and decorated appropriately. Mac also had a fantastic cake with the Hogwarts shield and other *Harry Potter* decorations. I really think he could hardly believe that this was all for him.

The village hall was full. In addition to Mac's godparents, their families, and all of our family, we also had close friends from the village and from work. These were all people who had been alongside us during the whole of the adoption process and before. We had organised a hog roast to feed everyone. The food went down well, with everyone having their fill of pork, stuffing, butcher's sausages, crackling, and salads. I had decided that this was the perfect time to make a speech, to mark the occasion and our happiness at becoming a family, and to thank all of the people there for their support and love over the years. I just about managed to get through the speech without cracking too much. But the real choker for everyone was about to come.

While we were preparing for the party, and talking Mac through what it would be like, he'd asked if he could say something. At first I was a little reticent, because I didn't want to put him in a position where he wanted to do something and then wasn't able to manage it. I was also unsure about what he might say! But we spoke to my best friend Adam (now one of Mac's godfathers) to ask if he would help him if he became too nervous. As it transpired, Mac *was* too nervous to make the speech, but he had written it, and in some ways it was all the more powerful with Adam delivering it. The words were all Mac's own. He put together a wonderful short speech, saying how much he had always wanted a family of his own and how happy he was to now be a part of ours. The words of his speech, exactly as written by Mac, are set out below:

Family

I wanted to be part of a family that looked after me and I had waited for eight and a half years to have a family like this. Before I came here I stayed with some special people called Sue and Mark and their family. Chelsea was there and was like me and we loved each other very much and she used to tease me. I loved to play with Archie who is the child of Sue and Mark's son Andrew and his wife Claire.

Richard and Swee are the right parents that I have been waiting for a long time to meet and now I am happy to live with them in St Mary Bourne because it is a nice quiet place.

They are nice kind people who care for me and love me. These are the family I have always wanted. Now I am going to sing a song.

Mac didn't sing a song! But his words did bring a round of applause. I know Swee and I were in tears – and we were not alone.

Mac's confirmation and my ordination

As I mentioned, I started my training about a year after Mac came to live with us. It did take up some of my spare time, but I was ruthless about how much time I spent away from Swee and Mac as I did not want our growing relationship to suffer – I tried to make sure I studied the minimum amount I could, and preferably when Mac was out doing other things or in bed. All of this study and training had to be done alongside my full-time job in Canary Wharf in London.

One of the things I had to do was go on a placement to another parish to see how things were in a parish different to our own. I picked a parish nearby in Newbury, and decided to look particularly at their successful youth work and what I could take from that. It was also a good opportunity to include Mac in my training as I could take him along and get his views on how the youth club worked and what he thought was good and bad – it would be interesting to have his perspective and give me the chance to be with him when I was away at this other parish. The parish is on the edge of Newbury, but had lots of families attending. This was something that they had really worked on, and they had built up a successful Sunday school during and after the main service for the children of parents who attended the church and others. They also ran a youth week during the first week of the summer holidays when they would work on a topic and do all sorts of exciting things: building arks, making costumes, and putting on a performance at the end.

So Mac and I went along to their services every Sunday for a couple of months. He loved it! He also met and made friends with another boy of a similar age to him. There was something about the welcome and the way in which children were treated in that church that was impressive. Actually, it also helped me to realise that the youth work that we did in our own church was pretty good, even if we did not have as many families and children as our village was much smaller than the catchment for the church in Newbury. The best thing was that Mac felt involved in my training. I asked him to write some material for my portfolio – it was good and showed an interesting take on what worked well with the youth work and what he didn't like. As ever, he was refreshingly honest.

All of this training finally led to my ordination, first as a deacon in July 2012, and then as a priest a year later. (As an aside, ordination is always to deacon level first. Deacons are not able to do all of the functions that a priest can do – e.g. deacons cannot take communion services or weddings. Then after a year, the majority of deacons choose to be ordained as priests.) Some of my favourite photos are of Swee, Mac and me on those ordination days. These took place at the end of June, and in Winchester Cathedral. It's a beautiful setting, and glorious in the early summer sunshine. We all look very happy. It is also amazing to see how much Mac grew in the year in between the two services.

Just a week or so before my ordination as a priest in 2013, Mac was confirmed at our church with the rest of his youth group. It was funny because he liked to make a point that he was being confirmed at much the same time as my ordination, and that both of these were done by our bishop. Mac had got to know our local bishop, David, as he had been around to our church a few times as we were in interregnum. This is the time of vacancy when one vicar has left and the next has not yet started in post. It is traditional in the Church of England for interregnum to last for at least a few months as part of the transition. In fact, by the time I was ordained we already knew who our new vicar was going to be. He was at that time one of the canons at Winchester Cathedral, and was in charge of organising the service of ordination.

Mac and Michael

Michael came to be our vicar in October 2013, a few months after my ordination. He had started to spend some time in the parish, and as he didn't have a family of his own we welcomed him into ours. We all immediately got on, and Mac and Michael particularly hit it off. Michael was fantastic with children and he never talked down to them. He had known a number of people who were adopted, and he immediately understood what Mac needed and how to treat him.

Michael had decided that he wanted to have servers at the altar. He believed that the best way to get children involved in the church was to give them jobs and responsibilities so that they felt part of what we were doing. Mac was very keen to be the first server, so we trained him up and got him the appropriate outfit. He was fascinated by all of the clerical outfits, and was always intrigued by my stoles and the fact that we would wear different ones at different times of the year: white for special occasions, green for ordinary Sundays, purple for Advent and Lent, and red for certain other festivals. So to go with his white cassock alb (the long white garment with a hood that our servers wore), he had different coloured rope belts to correspond with the liturgical seasons. It appealed to him. He used to go to church every week to serve, quite independently from me as I had to split my time between the four churches in our group. Michael taught him well and he became a very good server. He loved being in that church as he really felt a part of it. As well as having a real job to do, he was welcomed and treated well by everyone there.

In February 2014, just five months after Michael joined us, I got a phone call from my dad one evening to say that he had just been called over to the vicarage because Michael had just dropped dead from a massive heart attack. It was such a shock because he had been very well, and in fact it had been commented on by his old friends that he looked so much happier and more relaxed since he had left Winchester and moved to our village.

It is a testament to the man that he left so much of a hole in our lives after such a short time with us. He had established himself and become integrated with so much of the village already. For our family it was a particular tragedy as we had become incredibly close very quickly. Mac was devastated. He was very upset and angry.

Michael's funeral service was held at Winchester Cathedral. It was the most extraordinary service I have been to there, or anywhere. The place was packed, and all of the priests and bishops who had worked with and known him were sitting together in the sanctuary. The singing was the best I have heard. The Winchester Cathedral choir were sublime – they had worked with Michael for many years and they paid tribute to him in the only way they knew how. It might seem fanciful, but I have always believed that there are certain times when the gates of heaven are just a little bit open and we get a taste of that heavenly music – it certainly felt like it that day. The dean took the service and the Bishop of Winchester censed the coffin and blessed it with holy water.

That afternoon, we held the burial service at our local church as Michael had made it clear that he wanted to be buried in our churchyard. One of my colleagues led the much quieter service. He asked if Mac would like to carry the holy water to be sprinkled on the coffin and the grave. Mac was so pleased to be involved and to do his bit for Michael. A special place in the graveyard was found for Michael to be buried. There was a big space behind the church on its own, and Michael was laid to rest there. Mac and I solemnly followed the coffin with the holy water and incense as we recited the words of the Nunc Dimittis. It was a very moving service. Mac was amazing, although we hugged each other, very upset, afterwards.

A couple of weeks later, Michael's sister and brother-in-law came to visit. They had been clearing up Michael's affairs and sorting through his belongings. They knew that we had become close as a family, and that Mac was particularly sad to have lost him. They presented Mac with Michael's Bibles that he had been given at his ordination. They also gave him a knitted toy in the shape of Michael that one of his parishioners had given him some years before. Mac was very moved. The knitted Michael took pride of place in his bedroom, and I still have him safe today.

Mac (8) on his first visit to the village

Fun in the snow!

Mac, Swee and me having fun at a local party

There's nothing better than having fun in the sand – Cornwall (2010)

A Onesie for Christmas!

Such love

Thunder Mountain Disney World (2011)

The Magic Kingdom (2011)

A bucket list item for Swee – swimming with dolphins at Discovery Cove, Orlando (2011)

A tough day's fielding for the village team

Mac and Stella

Mac and me at my ordination at Winchester Cathedral (2013)

Mac dressed up as Harry Potter for World Book Day at school

Mac loved to help out. Here he is getting wet for the local duck race!

Mac sitting on the field now called Mac's Field in our village

Last school picture (and the best!)
(2016)

Sea fishing in North Carolina
(August 2016)

17 August 2016 – Mac's so proud of his bike for his 16th birthday.
No regrets, it gave him the freedom and independence he loved.

Mac at Murchison Falls in Uganda (February 2016)

Just some of the Floral tributes for Mac left at his school by his teachers and schoolmates

Chapter 11

Secondary School

Transition to secondary school

We knew that the transition to secondary school would be difficult for Mac. We had thought a lot about which school to send him to – as a formerly looked-after child, he would go to the top of all selection lists, so we did have a choice. However, the closest school was the school that I had been to and was just a short journey away on a school bus provided by the county. It was most convenient and most of Mac's friends would be going there. It had also been judged outstanding in its most recent Ofsted review. We had heard a number of worrying reports about bullying, but on balance it did seem like the best option.

We worked with Mac's primary school and the educational psychologist to make sure Mac was as ready as he could be. His new secondary school also worked with us to give him more opportunities to visit the school and be ready for the change. They also reassured us that there would be plenty of pastoral support: each of the houses to which the students belonged had a pastoral support assistant in addition to the school nurse, and pastoral support through the teaching staff. As he left primary school, we were sure that the best had been done to help Mac with the transition, so we enjoyed the school holidays and our summer holidays. We had bought his uniform and PE kit – all was ready.

The first day of school was kept just for the oldest and the youngest children. Mac walked to the bus stop in the village, just a couple of minutes' walk from our house, and got on the bus, ready for his first day. I had taken the day off work so that I was ready to see him when he came home in the evening, and make sure Swee and I were both around to support him.

It all seemed to go pretty well. Like all of the new year sevens, Mac was fairly daunted by having to move around the school to different classrooms for different lessons. Also, being Mac, he tended to dawdle a bit, so he was finding it difficult to make it to his lessons in time (though I'm not sure he was trying too hard). But it looked like it was OK – he knew who to go to for help and support if he needed it. We made sure early on to meet up with his form tutor and year head, and the pastoral assistant. We shared with them some of Mac's story and background so that they would be aware of and sensitive to any issues that might crop up over time.

Everything went OK to begin with. But Mac was spending quite a lot of time out of lessons for various reasons. He was still quite behind with his reading and writing, but he was being given help in class by classroom assistants. We met regularly with the school to assess progress and to help with issues as they arose. Mac was obviously struggling with some of the work. Worst of all was French. Luckily I had been pretty good at French, and could certainly remember enough to do year seven homework as competently as necessary, but I did begin to wonder if it was doing either of us any good!

Of course there were a few incidents as all of the students settled into school, and we did spend a little more time coming into school than some other parents. We had been warned that the transition was likely to be more difficult for Mac, as this is something that is often seen in children who have been in the care system. For Mac, the problems were always to do with forming relationships with his peers – he was still finding making those sorts of friendships difficult. And the change from spending time in one classroom to moving around a larger school with lots of different teachers was rather overwhelming for him. Although that is a big change for most children, his academic delays just made everything worse. But the school was dealing pretty well with Mac's problems and concerns, and helping him to start to feel like it was *his* school.

Then towards the end of the year Mac started to complain that he hated the school and wanted to move. We didn't take too much notice – we knew he was finding some aspects of school difficult, but we wanted him to persevere and stick it out. He had changed schools so much that we were keen that he had some consistency and didn't have to change schools again. We also felt that he was just finding things difficult and didn't want to work as hard as he was going to have to in order to be able to keep up.

On the positive side, he had met a good friend who lived nearby called Andrew. Andrew was also adopted and they had a huge amount in common. It was a good friendship and they supported each other. However, Andrew also struggled at times and just before the end of year seven his parents decided to take him out of school for a while to homeschool him. As you can imagine, Mac was devastated by this and clamoured to be homeschooled as well, but we knew that was not the answer for us or for him. We got to the end of the year with things going well, but on a bit of a downward trend. We welcomed the end of term and the start of the school holidays.

Year eight and onwards

We had a good summer holiday after year seven. Mac had a good rest and was fairly content to be returning to school. The increasing boredom of six weeks off always helped the start of term not seem too bad.

Things had changed at school. The old head had left and been replaced by one of her deputies, a very nice woman whom we knew and who knew Mac. Unfortunately, the assistant head who had been in charge of pastoral care had left and been replaced. He was a real loss as he had a fantastic touch with the children; particularly those who needed a little more care and attention. It soon became clear to us that pastoral care at the school was slightly in disarray. It wasn't that it wasn't still there; it was more that there was a lack of leadership.

Mac got back into lessons. Of course, they were getting more difficult and he was starting to struggle more. He was also having more trouble in the breaks. Without Andrew, he was struggling to make other close friends, and this made him more of a target. In hindsight, he was being bullied from an early stage – not necessarily physically as Mac was taller and stronger than any of them, but psychologically. There was lots of name-calling and teasing. Unwisely, Mac had shared his story with some of them, and they would use that against him, talking about his birth mum or saying things about us. Children can be very cruel, and find vulnerabilities easily and then use them mercilessly.

There had also been a change to the form structure. It was now a vertical structure with children from all years from the same house in each form. Although Mac was nominally assigned to one of these, it had been decided to put him in a special form group. This was made up of those children with special needs, and they met in the house on the grounds where special needs lessons were held.

Mac did come out of some lessons for help with English, but it is fair to say that he really hated it. Now a teenager and right in the middle of puberty, he wanted to fit in. He did not want to be singled out and treated differently. This accorded well with the way that we treated him. We had always resisted naming problems that Mac might have, instead working towards normalising him. We were pleased to be backed up by the school's educational psychologist who, when working with Mac, was clear that there were no real issues to be dealt with. Yes, he had missed a lot of early schooling and so was behind in basic reading and writing, and yes, he had suffered significant early neglect and that had left him with some remaining anger issues, but he was increasingly a 'normal teenager' (whatever that is), and was desperate to be treated that way.

But the school struggled with some of this. Swee was being called in more often, either to discuss a particular problem or to help out with a difficult incident. (I will leave it for a later chapter for Swee to describe the incident in the computing class!) Their way of dealing with Mac and any issues with his behaviour was to avoid dealing with them and to separate him from the boys he found it difficult to get on with.

Mac was also telling us how much he disliked the school. But he would still get up in the morning and go, and he did sometimes have good days. We wanted him to persevere and see it through as we thought he would feel much better for that.

A number of times I went in to see the head. I had looked into the other school that was most used by our village; a similar school in Winchester with a very good reputation. They were happy to take him. But on discussing it with our head, we agreed it would be better for Mac to see things through at his current school with their support.

Some of the confusion we had with our decision was due to the fact that Mac still appeared to be enjoying himself for some of the time, and lessons were not going too badly. The particular teacher for a subject always made a huge difference to Mac. In year eight, he suddenly started liking French and started to progress. This was all down to his teacher, Mrs Wales. It was clear that she also liked Mac and the relationship worked for him. It just went to show that a good teacher was able to support him and push him forward when it worked well. Most of the teachers warmed to Mac – they could see that he was desperate to be 'a good boy'. And the more they helped him to do that and to achieve, the better he succeeded.

In year eight there was a French trip to the Loire Valley. Mac was so excited about going, and spent lots of time planning what he wanted to take and imagining what it was going to be like. He was also excited because when there was a school trip, there was always a special T-shirt and hoodie available with a logo for that year's trip. Of course, these were partly for the teachers on the trip as they were better able to spot their students, but the added bonus was that on Fridays any official school hoodie from a trip with a sports team or club could be worn instead of the usual uniform. This was Mac's first opportunity to get one.

He had a fantastic time. The return ferry was running extremely late, and I remember sitting in the school car park in the early hours of the morning, ready to pick him up. The kids looked shattered as they got off the coach, but the teachers looked even more so! Mrs Wales came over to me specially to let me know how well Mac had done and how he had been a great support to some of the other students who were missing home – just as he had when he went on his primary-school trips. He had lots of stories to tell us about going shopping and all of the places they'd visited, and even trying out his French.

Sadly, Mrs Wales left at the end of that year as she was moving to a different part of the country. She asked to stay in touch with us and Mac to see how he was getting on. It's fair to say that his French went downhill drastically after that, and I had a lot more homework to do.

The final years

As Mac moved into year nine, he was able to choose some mini options to get him ready for when he would decide on his GCSE subjects for years ten and eleven. He made a few sensible choices which meant that he didn't have such an academic timetable. It turned out that Mac was remarkably good at needlework and he also enjoyed cooking, so there was the opportunity for him to do more of that. This also kept him away from some of the boys who were nasty to him.

But the school was still removing him from situations rather than dealing with them. They would openly agree that Mac was usually not at fault, but were unable to deal with what was in front of them. An example of this was the arrangements for PE. There were three groups in each year: the boys' group for the best boys, the girls' group for the best girls, and the mixed group for all of the others. Mac was put into the mixed group, even though he now stood head and shoulders above the other boys in his year (he was the oldest in the year, and tall for his age as well) and towered over the girls. He was also becoming a good sportsman as he was doing a lot of sport outside school: swimming, taekwondo and cricket. He hated being in the mixed group, and it meant he didn't get to try some sports or be considered for school teams. We complained and were backed up by the educational psychologist, and although the school promised to change things it never happened. It also seemed that he was not moved up in sets when he should have been – his maths teacher (again, a great teacher and one who 'got' Mac) felt that he was too good to be in the bottom set. But despite our best efforts, the move never happened.

Mac was increasingly being bullied in his free time. There was a group of boys who did their best to wind him up at every opportunity. Mac had become very good at getting himself out of situations, and we were always counselling him to just walk away and ignore them, but it was constant. The worst times were on the way to and from lessons. These were the real opportunities for the boys to know where he would be, and to get at him as he was queueing up, waiting to get into his next lesson. Not surprisingly, on a number of occasions Mac blew – and he always got the blame.

Towards the end of year nine, the incidences were increasing. Mac was telling us all the time that he was very unhappy and wanted to move. Finally, we could see that a move was becoming inevitable, and if we were going to do it, then it was best to do so before he started his GCSE options. We went to visit the head to talk about the problems as we saw them. Mac was so upset – he had been in trouble, and he broke down when we were in the head's study. He was so desperate to be good – he didn't want to get into trouble as he imagined his older brothers had – but he was finding it increasingly difficult to deal with the issues that he was facing.

Swee took him out to the car and I stayed to talk to the head. We had a good relationship, but it was clear that she did not have control of a cadre of the boys in the school. She admitted that she was not sure that she could keep Mac safe and out of trouble. We reluctantly agreed that a move was now in his best interests. We were literally at the end of summer term, but she promised to help facilitate the transfer to the Winchester school by writing to the head and calling her to assure her that everything would be OK. We were about to go on a cruise, and by the time we were due back the new school would be closed for the holiday. We all decided that Mac did not need to go back to school for the last few days, and we arranged to see the new head when we got back from holiday, just before the new term started.

Once the decision was made, Swee and I were actually quite relieved. The look on Mac's face was amazing: we saw all the worry and stress that had become ingrained lift away.

"I did try to tell you it was bad," he said.

But he did not bear a grudge. With perfect hindsight, we might have moved him earlier – we will never know if that would have been a better option. It certainly felt like the right decision for us all now.

Chapter 12

Growing Up

Sports and clubs

As Mac's parents, we wanted to make sure that he had as many opportunities to learn new skills and take part in new activities as he could, and to make up for some of the things he had missed out on in his earlier life. Academia was never going to be the highlight of Mac's life, so we wanted to find other areas that he could enjoy and excel in. We hoped that by joining clubs outside of school, he would also get the chance to meet new people and find a wider circle of friends.

We knew Mac loved the water, and as I mentioned earlier he had learned basic swimming in a week on holiday. He was very keen to have swimming lessons, so we signed him up for lessons at the local pool on Saturday mornings. During a previous placement Mac had also tried judo. Like many boys, he loved the idea of martial arts. We knew there was a fantastic taekwondo club at the same leisure centre as the pool, also on a Saturday morning, so it looked like we would be able to fit both in.

So, Saturday mornings became my time with Mac. I would take him to swimming lessons. He would then change for taekwondo and join the session after that. It worked extremely well. We normally rounded off the morning by having a quick lunch together – sometimes just a sandwich, or if we felt like a real treat, we might pop into the McDonald's drive-through.

Mac loved both of these activities. He was a strong swimmer from the beginning. Once he'd joined us, he'd begun to grow very, very quickly (as can be seen clearly by the markings on his bedroom wall where we recorded his height). He was in a constant growth spurt – in some way his body knew that he was happy and settled and responded accordingly. It was impossible to keep him in trousers that fit. He quickly moved up through the swimming classes as he learned the strokes and became stronger and stronger. Soon enough, he was moving into learning life-saving. As he was under sixteen, he could not qualify as a lifeguard. However, the swimming club ran a 'rookie lifeguard' qualification, and Mac steamed through this. He did so well in his swimming that the teachers asked him to stay on to join the next lessons so that he could help the younger, weaker swimmers.

We had been keen to look into taekwondo as we had heard such good things about the club and the black-belt instructor who ran it. He devoted an enormous amount of his time to the club, and to nurturing and teaching those who came. The emphasis was on balance, coordination and discipline – all things that Mac needed to work on. Just over a year before he came to us, he had broken his leg quite badly when his little brother jumped on top of him on a trampoline. He'd had to spend a long time in hospital, and although his leg had healed well, it had affected his balance. Mac loved taekwondo. He liked the challenge of the moves (or patterns) that he had to learn to gain the next belt up. He would stand proudly in the living room, showing us what he had learned and needed to practise. He gradually worked through his belts, and made it to blue belt. It was hard work, but he did enjoy his time at the club, especially when they spent some time working on sparring.

When it became too tough, Mac would often take a break for a while. We never forced him to go – we would encourage, but if he had decided, there was no point pushing it. In time he would go back and pick up where he'd left off. Sometimes I think he just needed a change from the routine.

The best thing for me about Saturday mornings was the time that we were able to spend together. After taekwondo class Mac would often say, "Can we take the long route back home?" This involved driving further out into the country and then driving back to our village through the valley. We would normally spend our time together in the car singing to the music we had on our phones, which we could play through the car stereo. We loved to sing together; often singing as loud as we could to the chosen track. A particular favourite was a song called 'JCB' by Nizlopi – just playing that now takes me straight back to those Saturday mornings.

We also used to talk in the car. There is something about sitting side by side, without the direct eye contact, that allows you to have a conversation that you might otherwise find too difficult. These were often the opportunities to find out if anything was particularly bothering Mac. We would also talk about his birth family and how he was feeling about them. As Mac grew up, we found that we needed to discuss issues that we'd thought had been dealt with when he was younger – of course, they had been dealt with appropriately, but as he grew and matured, he needed to deal with them again on a different level. For example, when he first came to us, when talking about his birth parents we would say that they hadn't been able to look after him. We might say that they had found it difficult to get their priorities right, but that of course they still loved him. As Mac grew older, he wanted to explore that further. He wanted more: why couldn't they put him first? Why had they neglected him? How were they now? Had they changed? It was often in the car that these difficult questions would arise. It caught me off guard at first, but I started to become more prepared to have these conversations. Of course, sometimes there was no answer, but we were able to discuss the issues in a mature way and help him to process them. Sometimes the questions were triggered by something that had been discussed at school – when drugs were discussed in his PSE classes that inevitably sparked a number of thoughts and questions. What Swee and I were always keen to do was to make sure that he knew he could come to us with any question and we would not be shocked or fazed. I think we normally managed.

Growing up in the village

One of the things that you are asked to do when you are going through the adoption approval process is to sit down and map out your support network – it is vitally important that you have people around you who can help you through the transition, especially as first-time parents.

Adopting a child, rather than a baby, means that you go from nought to 100 immediately! An eight-year-old child moves into your lives as a talking small human being, with opinions, behaviours and attitudes that have been built up over the past eight years – eight years that are basically a complete mystery to you as their new parents. There is no shared history at this point, so you have to try harder to understand why your child is behaving in a certain way.

One of the advantages is that your child is able to talk and try to explain what is going on; clearly something a newborn baby cannot do. So it's good to be able to find ways to have conversations and discussions with your child (at the appropriate level) to begin to understand and piece together their past. Social workers will have filled in some of the gaps for you, but it is inevitable that there will be much more to come out as your child feels more comfortable. And what we found was that it was important not to react in a shocked way to any disclosures. Swee and I both became very good at maintaining a poker face. We wanted Mac to feel comfortable to tell us anything at all.

I'm sure that much of this is the same when bringing up any child – but normally you will have had a few years to get to know them and their character and quirks. With adoption, those are present from day one.

When we did our mapping, we first of all noted down all of our family – we knew they would be our primary support. We also had friends with similar-aged children who would be there for advice and help. As we considered the wider context, we began to realise just how much the village itself was an enormous source of support. As the proverb goes, 'It takes a village to raise a child.' For us this worked on so many levels. Not only did we have a wonderful local GP surgery that practised the best family care, but there were all sorts of other communities, such as the church and clubs, that were there to support us. I had moved to the village when I was twelve and my parents ran the local pub. Many of the villagers had seen me grow up. They knew me and Swee really well, and they had lived through our struggle to have a family. They were now looking forward to supporting us in the next stage.

Having said that, it was a double-edged sword. As I have mentioned before, some people expected us to be more open about Mac's past. There was nothing to hide, but it was his past to share. When we didn't share it, all sorts of false assumptions were made. With a village comes a lack of privacy: it is almost impossible to do anything without someone knowing. An example of this was when we first moved into our new house and replaced the kitchen. The kitchen window looked out over the main road, and one evening we were at a dinner party when someone told us how much they loved our new kitchen, especially our Smeg fridge – they had not been invited in (we didn't know them that well), but had clearly had a good look through the window, and were keen to voice their opinion!

All of this meant that there was plenty of support for us and for Mac, even if it was next to impossible to work through any issues in private. On balance, I'd rather have it that way.

Mac was generally popular with the adults in the village. We let him have freedom to go to the local shop and the recreation ground just a five-minute walk away. The joy of the village was that our children were much safer than they would be in a town. Mac used to love to get around on his scooter – he was still perfecting the skills he'd tried to show us when we'd first met. He got through many scooters: at least one every birthday and Christmas for a couple of years. He really was 'Scooter Boy'. He also had a number of bikes – both BMX and mountain bikes, assuring us that they were needed for different things. To be fair, he did use them a lot and didn't ask for much else, so we were happy to get them for birthday or Christmas presents.

Our village has an annual flower show and fete. This is a traditional affair, in which a large marquee is put up each year and villagers proudly exhibit their various flowers and vegetables, culinary delicacies, and artwork in the hope of winning prizes. The glory is in the honour, not the prize money, which was at most £1. Swee and I had done our bit over the years. I had some success with my bread – especially my flavoured Mediterranean loaf – and Swee had won prizes with her photos. She had less luck with her flower arranging: although they were always beautiful, they were sometimes a little avant-garde for the visiting judges, who knew exactly what they liked. A comment one year on Swee's choice of flowers for her 'posy in a jam jar' was "Lovely choice of colours, but flowers a little large for a petite"!

There were also plenty of special children's classes, so for Mac's first flower show we helped him to get involved and enter lots of them. The best class was for a miniature garden, for which a special cup was awarded. Mac won on his first attempt (with only a little input from Swee). He actually enjoyed it and did have a good eye. He also won some prizes with his biscuits and photos. One class asked for an edible animal. The intention was for the kids to make funny animals from misshapen vegetables – but this was not made clear. So Swee and Mac made a fantastic elephant cake – Mac always baked beautiful-tasting cakes. The judges awarded him a begrudging third prize, but did point out that it wasn't what they had intended. There was also a fancy dress competition. At the last minute, Mac and Emily (my nephew's daughter) decided they wanted to enter. Mac wanted to be a pirate and Emily wanted to be a princess. We scrabbled about for bits and pieces and, much to our shock, they both won. Mac loved that flower show, and as well as the money he won, he also had to go up and receive the cup for his miniature garden. He was very proud.

As Mac grew older, he got involved in a number of village activities. First of all, he started going along to the cricket club. He enjoyed this as he and his friend Andrew used to go along together. They would practise in nets during the week. The club was always keen to encourage the younger villagers, and always looking for players for the Sunday team, so the boys would often get a game. Of course, with practice and encouragement, they got better and better.

The village also had an annual duck race down the small river to raise money for the village shop. Hundreds of numbered yellow plastic ducks would be thrown into the river. Previously, the ducks would have been sold, and the duck that won the race would win a prize. Of course, these ducks were used again and again every year, so it was important to be able to retrieve them all. A couple of people would walk down behind the ducks, encouraging them along and releasing the ones that were caught in the undergrowth. Mac and a couple of other guys would then be positioned at the end of the race route, dressed in waders, with a large net across the stream to ensure that all of the ducks were caught and accounted for. I have great pictures of Mac in his waders, working away. It was hard work, but he was particularly well suited to it as he was growing so tall.

Mac was probably one of the best customers of our village shop – saving was not a concept that he understood and he loved to go and spend his pennies on various treats. Also, if we needed anything, he loved to go for us. However, if I gave him a £10 note he had an incredible knack of spending the whole thing. He didn't like to bring back any change. So it was probably inevitable that he started volunteering and working in the shop as he got older; first helping them with the shelves and then working on the till. He loved working there. Mac was always positive and friendly, so it gave him the perfect opportunity to meet and chat to people. Of course, it also kept him nice and close to the sweets and crisps that he could spend his hard-earned pennies on!

The village was, and is, the perfect place to bring up children. It has the best combination of friendship, companionship, and plenty of people to look out for you. The village really did help to bring Mac up and support him as he grew into a wonderful, mature young man.

Dressing up

I mentioned the pirate costume earlier, but Mac loved to dress up more generally. He liked nothing better than to put together a costume and play to his heart's content.

There were a few fancy dress parties that we went to. Mac looked particularly good as a gangster for one of those (the year before, over a week he had enjoyed putting on *Bugsy Malone* with a summer holiday club). He also dressed up a few times for World Book Day at school. He made a perfect Harry Potter – he had just the right look. And one year Swee dressed him up in a toga for Greek Day when they were learning about ancient Greece. He also dressed up one year as a Roman centurion.

He loved to dress up in suits and ties, too – he liked nothing better than to be smart (something that was hard to imagine when he came in from school having played muddy football during the breaks). I can also remember one Christmas when he paraded around in his Union Jack onesie we had just bought him, pretending to show off his muscles like a bodybuilder.

But one costume stands out for me above every other, and it was one he put together for himself on a bored afternoon. We were suspicious because we could hear various noises from his bedroom as he rummaged around, looking for the things he needed. When he came down he looked amazing. He had decided he wanted to look like Harry Potter playing Quidditch. He had dressed up in a football jersey. He had put football pads on his arms and legs. He had a long piece of cardboard as a broom, and a ball to throw. Of course, this was all topped off with his Harry Potter glasses. He looked brilliant! He enjoyed posing for pictures and pretending to play Quidditch. He loved to use his imagination so much, and dressing up was always a great outlet.

TV and films

I can't talk about Mac's growing up and his interests without mentioning TV and films.

Like most children, he liked to watch TV. When he was younger he enjoyed the Disney Channel and Nickelodeon. He watched all of the series; particularly *Hannah Montana*, *The Suite Life of Zack & Cody*, and *Phineas and Ferb*. His favourite was *Wizards of Waverly Place*, and we often used to sit down and watch it together. Mac would happily watch the same episode again and again.

We used to watch TV together in the evening. Swee and Mac always watched *EastEnders* together. (Actually, we often found it brought up useful subjects that we could then discuss with him.)

We also loved to watch the typical Saturday-evening programmes together, like *Merlin* or *Atlantis* and particularly *Doctor Who* – great family entertainment. As Mac got older, he watched TV with us less, as he could stream series on his tablet, or watch TV in the kitchen. But he still loved a series, especially enjoying *Casualty* and *Holby City*.

But more than TV, I think Mac loved films. He and I would often go to the cinema at the weekend or during the holidays, to see the latest releases and enjoy a frozen slush drink and jelly sweets. We also had loads of DVDs at home. Of course, we watched the *Harry Potter* and *Lord of the Rings* films time and time again. Swee and Mac would often sit down and watch a DVD together if he had done his homework and wasn't going outside to play.

I remember fondly a story Swee recounted to me one day when I got home from work. One of Mac's favourites was the remake of *St Trinian's* – the humour appealed to him. After watching it one time, he asked Swee, "Mum, what's a Brazilian?" She knew he wasn't referring to the nationality! So, she valiantly explained the finer details of that particular form of hair removal. He seemed satisfied with the explanation and carried on watching the film.

Without doubt, Mac's favourite film was *Forrest Gump*. He watched it for the first time on a cruise on a day when the weather wasn't as nice. We were snuggled up in the cabin and it was on the film channel. I have to admit, I had never seen the film either. Mac was hooked. Something about the character of Forrest chimed with him. He watched the film again and again, and nearly wore out the DVD at home. He knew it back to front, and did a wonderful impression of Forrest.

Mac knew he wasn't academic, and for that reason particularly liked to use the quote, about not being smart, but knowing what love is. It's hard to argue with that sentiment.

Chapter 13

New School, New Start

The summer holidays

Once we had made the decision to move schools there was not much more that we could do. We were about to go on holiday, and by the time we returned, the school would be shut for the summer. There was just enough time to order some new school uniform and for the two head teachers to exchange letters and agree, in principle, that the transfer could go ahead. As I have mentioned before, the useful thing about any child who has been previously looked after by the state, even if they are now adopted, is that they will normally go to the top of the preference list of any state school. We also knew that there were spaces at the school. We made arrangements to meet the head teacher just before the start of the new autumn term to agree classes and options for Mac's GCSE subjects.

There were a few days before the end of term, and we had agreed that there was no need for Mac to return to his old school – he was not bothered about saying goodbye as he had become so unhappy and was looking forward to a few more days' break before we went on our holiday. Of course, rumours were rife around school, and therefore also around the village. Lots of people were convinced that Mac must have been expelled. We had found in the past that it was best just to ignore these sorts of rumours. Of course, our friends and family knew the truth, and if anyone bothered to check their facts with us, then we would be able to tell them as well. As ever, the less we commented, the quicker the rumours ebbed away and the gossips found someone else to talk about.

It had been a difficult year for various reasons. Swee's mum and dad had died within a week of each other in February. They were both in a home and Swee's mum had suffered with Parkinson's for thirty years, but there had been no warning that either of them was that ill. Their loss hit all of us hard – Mac had been very upset at the funeral as he had been extremely close to both of them. Swee had spent more and more time looking after her parents over the past few years, and she started to get ill after they died – she mourned them physically, rather than emotionally. What with this, and the increasing problems Mac had been having at school, we were ready for a holiday. We were ready for our Mediterranean cruise – the three of us were going with Swee's brother. It was going to be a wonderful break.

Unfortunately, it didn't turn out quite as we had hoped. Just a day or so into the cruise, Swee was really sick and suffering the most enormous pain. The on-board doctors were fairly sure it was a kidney stone and wanted her to have it checked out ashore. Once we docked in Gibraltar, she and I rushed to the local hospital – we had to race against time to have Swee scanned before the boat left with Andy and Mac on board. And we needed the scan to confirm the diagnosis before the doctors on board would be happy to treat Swee, and not insist she stayed ashore to be flown home. With just half an hour to go we got back to the boat, with scans showing that the stone was too big to either pass or get stuck, and so she could be treated with pain medication until we got home. If anyone had been watching us that day, they would have seen two mad-looking holidaymakers squeezing into the smallest taxi to ensure we could get back to the ship in time, and me running with Swee in a wheelchair onto the gangplank. She was feeling much better now; partly from relief, I think. We both decided we needed a nice cold cocktail once we got back.

The rest of the cruise was fairly uneventful, if a little boring for Swee as she was not feeling particularly energetic and was advised to rest. But Andy, Mac and I made the most of our time on the boat and on visits ashore, and generally had a good time.

Just after we got back home Mac and I went for the meeting with the new school head. She was very welcoming. I immediately felt a different approach compared with Mac's previous school: this school had an emphasis on getting the very best from their students, and an impressive record for student performance, comparing well with all other Hampshire schools. It was clear that they wanted students to succeed, but that was not measured by attainment alone, but rather by the amount by which they had improved. We discussed the options that Mac could take. He was excited as he was able to take engineering as a GCSE, and he also decided to do music and RE. He was much relieved that he was not expected to take a foreign language (as was I, as I had become bored with French homework!). All was prepared, and a few days later Mac left the house (earlier as the journey was further, and the school day started sooner) dressed in his new uniform, ready to catch the minibus to his new school. A new era had begun.

New friends

Starting at a new school after everyone else has settled in is never easy. I had to do that when I moved to Hampshire at the age of twelve, and I had wanted to avoid this for Mac. I think that had probably delayed our decision to look at moving him before. Yet it was a good move for various reasons:

- It gave him a completely clean slate with teachers and students.
- Some of the students knew him from the village, but he would be able to decide how much of his past he revealed, and to whom.
- He was more confident in himself than he had been at the age of eleven when he'd started at his previous school.
- He really wanted to make this work.
- The school ethos worked better for Mac.

This showed itself in lots of ways. Mac had become much happier in his own skin. He was more confident with his peers, and able to make friends much more easily. He was very caring and was able to spot those in need of help, and they seemed to be attracted to him – he was often sought out for his advice.

Mac had also grown up physically. He was now well over six foot tall, and looking forward to the day when he would finally overtake me in height and become the tallest in our family. As he was very active and doing a fair amount of sport outside school, he had also become lean and strong. He was developing into a good-looking young man – he was not as aware of this as we were, though, and was slightly surprised by the attention he got. It was clear that the girls were intrigued by this tall, dark, mysterious, handsome stranger who had turned up in their midst. Mac would say to me, "This girl kept staring at me today, Dad!" Swee and I would just laugh and tell him that maybe she fancied him. Every couple of weeks or so, he mentioned the names of different girls who were taking an interest. It seemed that his popularity was likely to be assured.

Mac was also making friends. He asked to stay behind after school to go round to friends' houses – something he had rarely done at his old school. And there was no mention of bullying at all. He spoke of school much more warmly – it felt like he was taking ownership and properly feeling part of the school in a way that he had never been able to do before. We had taken a risk in making the move, but it was proving successful in every way.

New lessons

The approach that the school took with Mac was completely different and accorded much more with the way that we treated him and the way that he wanted to be treated. Rather than removing him from classes to help him out, they ensured that he was part of the normal classes and any help he needed was provided there. In fact, the more he was treated as 'normal', and the more the teachers expected him to be able to keep up, the more he actually managed to do that. They didn't give him an easy excuse not to try and succeed, and consequently he started to succeed more. I remember early on when I was speaking to the head asking whether she thought Mac would be able to achieve passes in the basic subjects like maths, English and science – something that had not been assured or necessarily expected of him before.

"I sincerely hope so!" she said, looking at me as if I had somehow taken leave of my senses.

They believed in him and put the time into him, and consequently he began to believe in himself.

Mac was doing much better at school. He started to move up in maths – he had always been better at maths. But he also started talking more about English, and having conversations about some of the books he was studying for his exams. He still struggled with his spelling, but his writing was now good, and at least his spelling was now understandable even to the uninitiated. It became clear that spelling was never going to be his forte, but he was at least able to write faster and clearer, which meant he could get his thoughts down in a more coherent manner.

For the first time in a long time, Mac began to enthuse about certain subjects in school. He loved engineering. He spent lots of time on his engineering homework projects, researching materials and designs and working on his drawings. He had become so much more precise. He produced a wonderful piece of work for a home alarm project, and we could see how much he enjoyed all aspects of the process.

He also enjoyed RE. RE is compulsory as part of the national curriculum, but not all students studied it for GCSE. Mac did, and enjoyed it. Of course, he had a good background in Christianity, being a priest's son (something of which he now appeared to be quietly proud), and all those hours sitting in the church choir and listening to Michael meant that a huge amount of information had gone in. Like me, he was also fascinated by other religions and their similarities and differences. The other large part of RE was learning to discuss moral and philosophical topics. Mac would come home having had a discussion on contraception, abortion or same-sex marriage, and love to talk through the issues. On one occasion he called me on my mobile during the lesson. Luckily, although I was at work, I was at my desk. He wanted me to talk to the class over the phone to explain a particular issue to do with the church. I did the best I could, but I could see members of my department looking at me in a fairly strange way.

That is not to say that all was rosy. Mac struggled with music. Part of the course required him to write and perform a piece of music and be able to explain the process and the thoughts behind it. Although he did have a nice voice, and was happy to belt out a song when it was just him and me in a car, he was much more embarrassed in class. He had also been learning the drums before and was now taking guitar lessons. He was improving, but didn't have the commitment to sit down for the hours of practice that were really necessary to get good. Consequently, he was falling behind in his project, which was to form part of his final exam mark. Previously he had been able to get away with avoiding things, having only rarely been picked up on these issues. The difference at his new school was that nothing was allowed to slide. I was called in by his music teacher to discuss how we could help to get him back on track. She offered much of her own time to help him, as long as he knuckled down. I knew the behaviour of old – if Mac thought he was failing at something, he would often stick his head in the sand and hope it would go away. If he didn't try, then he would not fail. Now, that was not an option – he was not allowed to avoid anything, but would be helped to make sure that he did his best in everything. The approach in the school was fantastic.

I was also impressed by the behaviour of the students. As ever, there were one or two occasions when Mac started to get into trouble. He could still be a bit of a loner at times, and as such was sometimes a target. Again, the approach was completely different. Whereas at his old school there had been a lack of control of some behaviour during breaks, here the teachers were always on top of things. It wasn't that the grounds were easier to patrol – if anything, I think they were a little more difficult. The staff just had a good sense of what was going on. I remember speaking to the head about it once, when she had stopped a group of boys ganging up on Mac. She said, "I always spend some time outside during breaks, and I have a sense if something isn't right. The other day when I walked past the group of boys with Mac, I had a strong feeling that something was awry, so I turned back and caught the start of it and was able to discipline those responsible." At Mac's old school, they wouldn't have got there until something had happened, and normally Mac would have been blamed. That was why they lost his trust. His new head knew her school, and knew when things were working or not. This approach was mirrored in her staff. It was, and is, a very impressive school.

I could tell how much happier Mac was. He was more ready to talk about school, and I remember laughing much more with him. One day he came home to tell me that they had done an exercise at school so that they would know what to do if someone attacked the school or if they needed to shelter. On the command, they had to get under their desks and hide and protect themselves. As Mac explained, the teachers hadn't allowed for someone like him, who was at least six foot three by now. Laughing, he said, "I would have been an easy target because my head was left sticking out the top!" With that, he proceeded to dive under his desk in his bedroom to show how difficult it was. I can still remember laughing for ages, with Mac's fantastic laugh ringing in my ears.

School sports

Sport was also a huge success for Mac at his new school. His head of year was a PE teacher and took an immediate shine to him, and Mac liked him. He saw Mac's potential and began to get him involved in all sorts of sports. As it was winter term, Mac started with football and rugby. He was OK at football, but there were plenty of boys faster and nimbler than him who had been playing competitive football for a long time. But the school was good at rugby, and they could see that Mac's height and strength were going to be hugely useful in their team.

So, he started to play school rugby. He did enjoy it – he was fast enough. But he was best as a forward, bringing real strength to the scrum. I started to have to pick him up late from school after a rugby match on a number of occasions. He also made some friends in the team. There was one downside to rugby for Mac. When he was younger he had been fearless. As he was growing older, like many of us, he was becoming slightly more reticent to throw himself into more physical situations. He knew it was going to hurt and had decided he didn't like it. As a forward, it was inevitable that he would spend a lot of the time crunching into other big bodies – and despite his clear aptitude for the game, after the season was over he decided that his rugby career was also going to end.

Luckily, next came cricket. This was a game that Mac loved. As he practised a lot in the village he was getting better. With some good teaching at school, he began to improve and again was chosen for the school team. His PE teacher recounted to me the time when Mac had taken his first wicket for the school. He said that the look on his face was so fulfilling as a teacher, and one that he would never forget – Mac had responded so well to their belief in his abilities. At the prize-giving at the end of the year, Mac was stunned to receive a prize as the most improved cricketer. He hadn't won a prize at school since he'd left primary school.

As the summer approached, we reflected on the huge change in Mac over the past year. Changing schools had been the making of him. He was happier, more mature, more grown-up, and working hard. He was succeeding at sports and was on track to do the best that he could in his exams. Most of all, he was happy.

What a difference a year can make!

Chapter 14

Pets, Friends, Girlfriends and Growing Older

Pets

Swee and I always had pets. We got our first dogs, Rigby and Peller the Cavalier King Charles Spaniels, as wedding presents, so they were with us from the beginning of our married lives. Before we were married we both had cats and loved having them around, and I know neither of us could imagine a house without animals to share it with us.

Mac also loved animals. He had loved Sue and Mark's Golden Retriever. So when he'd come to live with us he'd soon come to love our dogs, and they loved to snuggle up with him on the sofa. However, they never really played with him quite as much as he would have liked – they preferred to snooze the day away. But they were always good for a cuddle.

For his first pet, we decided Mac could have the hamster he had been asking for. I'm not sure Mac knew much about hamsters, but I think he felt it was the sort of pet that you could ask for when you had a new family. We set off for Pets at Home, chose the appropriate modular cage, bought all of the food, bedding and treats that we needed, and then went to choose the hamster. As ever, there were a few possibilities. Mac chose one and we started for home. We put everything together and let the hamster into her cage – Mac decided she should be called Lizzie.

Lizzie was a very typical-looking hamster with the normal markings and sandy colour, but she had red eyes. Mac decided he didn't like these – it was not a good start to the bonding of hamster and boy! I started to help him get to know Lizzie and how to pick her up (I had hamsters when I was younger, so was fairly sure I knew what I was doing). At this point Mac was still a bit clumsy, but he was ready to be very gentle with Lizzie. However, try as we might, Lizzie did not like any human contact – we would leave her to calm down and give her some treats, and then try again. On one occasion we got close to picking her up but she jumped out of our hands and fell on the floor. Luckily, she was unharmed, but stunned, and I was able to scoop her up and put her back in the cage. We must have had the unfriendliest hamster in England. We were nearly bitten a number of times. To be fair, I think she had been rather old when we got her and she was past being happy to be domesticated.

One day I had a call at work from Swee, saying, "I don't think Lizzie is very well. She has a large growth coming out of her bottom!"

"Are there two growths?" I asked.

"Yes."

"Well, I think we're going to have to call Lizzie, Les!"

Swee had never seen a mature male hamster, so was surprised by the size of his testicles. I was glad I wasn't going to have to find a way to get her (or more strictly, him) to the vet.

Lizzie (the change of name never really stuck) lived out her days very happily. She had a huge cage and plenty of room to run around. We cleaned her out every week and she had all the food, water and treats a hamster could have. I think she got the better half of the deal. Not surprisingly, when Lizzie did eventually make her way to hamster heaven, she was not replaced.

Mac's next significant pet was Ron the cat. We'd decided it was time to get another cat. Mac and I saw a litter advertised and found out that there were kittens left. We went to choose, under strict instructions from Swee that with the two dogs we only needed one cat. Needless to say, we came home with Ron (a beautiful ginger tom) and Hermione (a grey tabby version of Ron). Swee, of course, fell in love with them instantly. The two cats were very different: Hermione was much braver and more 'catlike' than Ron. Ron was a complete softie. But very soon we realised that he had a problem: he was dribbling urine everywhere! This led to him having to have an operation to remove all of his 'boy's bits' (yes literally all of them!), but at least he was now clean.

Ron and Mac had an amazing relationship. They used to play football together, with Ron batting a small ball around with Mac. He would follow Mac everywhere; particularly into choir practice in the church. Ron became quite the regular churchgoer! If we walked over to my sister's house about five minutes away, he would often come along with us. The best thing about Ron was that he would come whenever he was called, especially if it was Mac calling. Even if Ron was out and about, if Mac called, suddenly he would be there, having come back from wherever he had been scouting around. Mac loved Ron and Ron loved Mac.

One day when I was at work, Swee called in tears – poor Ron had been hit by a car on the road in front of our house. Some friends of ours had taken him away, but he had been killed outright. I got home and Mac and Swee were inconsolable – Ron was just two years old. We had lost other cats on the road, so we decided: no more cats.

As I said, our dogs were getting very old, and were not much fun for a lively teenager. Eventually we agreed that we would get a puppy, if Mac promised to look after her. We had looked into breeds and (knowing that despite his best intentions, Mac probably wouldn't walk her every day) decided to get a Cavachon – a cross between a Cavalier and a Bichon Frise. They have the wonderful nature of the two parents, are fairly relaxed and very friendly, and usually don't shed. Perfect! So in April 2015, Swee, Mac, Andy and I went to choose our new puppy.

We arrived at the breeder's house and the litter was brought out to us. There were only bitches left, which was fine as we were fairly sure that our old dogs would take more easily to a female. I had seen a picture of the litter before we went, and so was expecting to choose the apricot puppy. Sure enough, she came bowling out and demanded attention. Then just behind her came a beautiful sable-and-white puppy. She was confident as well, but not quite as boisterous as her apricot sister. Mac picked her up and she immediately snuggled in. It was clear: the sable-and-white puppy was coming home with us. Mac named her Stella.

When we got home, she soon settled in – she loved to snuggle up with the older dogs when she was tired. Once she'd had all of her injections, Mac started taking her out for walks. We also booked her in for Kennel Club-approved puppy training classes. Every Sunday after church, I would drive Mac to the class and he would go in by himself to the training. It was a great way for him to learn about training a dog, and he and Stella formed the closest bond from then. She loved to be with him, sitting on his lap while he watched TV if he let her. Mac had always said he wanted a Staffie, but we knew he did not have the determination to exercise a Staffie as much as it would need. Stella was just right: she would love to go for a walk with him, but was content if he wasn't in the mood. Despite his occasional protests, it was clear he adored her and was proud of her whenever he took her out. His training really made a difference: she was (and still is) the best-trained dog that we have had. Mac and Stella were the best of friends.

Significant friendships

Mac struggled with friendships with his peers. Having moved so often in his life, he never had the chance to learn how to make friends and the realities of being a friend. To begin with he would often be too 'full-on', and he would also make bad judgements about how his peers felt about him. Once he had started to make a friend, when inevitably they fell out over something trivial, Mac would find that incredibly hard to deal with. For one, he was unfailingly loyal and couldn't understand why they might not feel quite the same. Also, he had never had the chance to have friends for long enough to understand that friends can fall out, but still be friends. He had never been somewhere long enough to make a friendship that had weathered the ups and downs.

In contrast, Mac was fantastic with younger children. He had looked after his little brother a lot while they were together, and naturally had always felt very protective of him. Now that they no longer lived together, he often tried to replace that relationship. He would ask us if we would adopt a younger brother or sister. On one level, we would have loved a larger family, and had always envisaged having two children. But the approval process had been so unpleasant, intrusive and badly managed that we didn't feel we could go through it again as a family. Mac had a really close friendship with his teacher's young son, who started at primary school when Mac was in year five. They got on very well, and Mac enjoyed playing the older brother role – it was a role that he was very good at.

He was also great with adults. While the constant moves in his life had affected his relationships with peers, they had improved his relationships with adults. Of necessity, he had learned to ensure that he got on with adults and endeared himself to his various carers. He was naturally charming, but had clearly become adept at reading certain clues, and consequently usually got on very well with the adults with whom he came into contact.

An example of this occurred one weekend when Mac and I had gone up to Nottingham to see my best friend Adam and his family (Swee stayed behind to look after the dogs). Mac really enjoyed Adam's company. Adam has a huge garden, and was planting out 100 conifer saplings. He and Mac went out to plant them, while I stayed in the warm, chatting to Adam's wife, Lindsay. Mac liked to have the chance to have one-on-one time with other people, without his dad interfering! They worked fantastically hard that afternoon and planted all of the conifers. Sadly, not all of the trees survived, as Adam told us when he was next at our house. Mac's only response, with a wry grin, was, "I hope you don't think I'm going to plant any more for you!"

Mac did make some good friends when at school. At primary school he became best friends with Bailey. They were well matched. Bailey was also new to the school and the village, so they naturally gravitated to one another. It gave them both some confidence in school, as the boys' group was already a bit cliquey. They had all been together since they'd started school (and some of them for longer), so their bonds were deep. Bailey and Mac used to play a lot after school. Swee got on very well with Bailey's mum, so they both managed to 'run the gauntlet' of playground politics, basically by staying out of it and being in the background. It's fair to say that without Bailey and his brother, Connor, Mac would have found primary school much more difficult. Sadly, the family left the village before the end of primary school. Mac missed them, and they did still meet up from time to time, but they certainly got him through the more difficult early years.

It's not that Mac didn't get on with the other children. He did. But his behaviour had been more challenging when he'd first moved into the school and they only had so much patience. Also, some boys can be a bit competitive, and Mac was seen as competition. He got on better with the girls, and certainly had easier friendships with them, which endured past primary school.

School can be difficult, especially when it comes to parties. Earlier on there were a couple of occasions when the whole of Mac's class was invited to a birthday party, except him. I know these things can be difficult, but as a parent, it is devastating to see your child missed out in such an obvious way. We were thrilled when Mac was invited to his first birthday party – it was a Laser Quest party and he had a fantastic time. There were a few parents who definitely gave him the benefit of the doubt a little more, and I am forever grateful to them – these small gestures make such a significant difference.

Mac's best friend was definitely Andrew, whom I mentioned in the chapter on secondary school. Even after Andrew moved school, he and Mac spent lots of time together. They were always going off on their bikes and riding around the area. They had sleepovers in our garage and spent loads of time just hanging out. Simply put, they understood and looked out for each other. I think there was real care there, with neither of them wanting the other to be hurting in any way. Of course, they fell out from time to time, but as real friends do, they were able to come through those things.

I remember when they were fifteen, they camped out near where Andrew lived, which was in a hamlet near us. I knew there was illicit alcohol and probably tobacco stashed away – I wasn't surprised; I had done the same thing when I was their age. But Mac didn't try to hide things: he showed us the photos he took, and they were very bleary-eyed and stunk of beer in the morning. They still managed to eat their bacon.

Girlfriends and growing up

Mac was a very good-looking boy and, as he grew taller and stronger, became something of a catch. (I feel I can say this as I had nothing to do with his genetics!) But when he came to us he was totally innocent: it was some time before he realised that girls were taking notice of him. His low self-esteem meant he didn't understand that they might like him. As he was growing up, we were always telling him how handsome he was – partly as a bit of fun, but also to subtly improve his view of himself.

But apart from sending a Valentine's card to one of his friends, there was no romance on the horizon. When Mac was about fourteen, he did start hanging round with one of the girls in the village. She was new – in fact, her family had moved into Bailey's family's house.

She and Mac got on very well, and she had the knack of calming him down if he got angry. Mac's temper was much more under control now, and the incidences lasted much less time. He would normally get angry because we had stopped him from doing something he wanted to do – pushing against those boundaries again. But there was no real romance in this relationship as such. She was a year or so older than Mac and had a boyfriend. However, Mac did like to buy her presents – she was really a close friend on whom he could try out his embryonic flirting. When he moved schools they grew apart as he made more friends nearer Winchester. Sadly, they then had a big falling-out, which was never properly resolved.

Mac was now growing up. He was becoming a little more distant with us, as is natural for a teenager, I think. He was certainly more secretive at times. But we always made sure that he knew that the door was open and that we would always support him and love him, even if he made a mistake. We know that he dabbled with weed: it was rife among many of the teenagers, for whom it had replaced alcohol as the drug of choice. We found some evidence of that, and talked to him. He was honest, and we talked the issue through. He knew the dangers more than most as he had seen how drugs could destroy a family. It never became a huge issue.

He was talking more to his birth family as well. This was natural as he was looking forward to when he would be free to have more direct contact with them. He had a mature attitude to the ways in which they had let him down, but Mac was so loving and forgiving – I think this was one of his nicest traits. You can never forget when you have an adopted child (especially one adopted at an older age) that the birth family will often still play a part in their life.

We were always supportive and told him we would always help him and be there for him.

A few months after starting at his new secondary school in autumn 2015, Mac got his first proper girlfriend. They were both fifteen and had a sweet friendship. They used to spend time at each other's houses, taking it in turns. We would also take it in turns to ferry them around. Sometimes we would drop them off in town and they would go to the cinema and maybe pop to McDonald's. It was a typical 'first girlfriend/boyfriend' relationship. They learned a lot from each other about how to treat members of the opposite sex, and it ran its course after a couple of months.

As we approached 2016, Mac was looking forward to turning sixteen in August. He was keen to get a motorbike – I was not keen, and encouraged him to wait for a year until he could get a car. I said I was happy to buy him a car when the time came, but not a motorbike. Discussions continued as 2016 came closer.

Then came Amy. We didn't know much about her except that he told us about her just before we went on holiday to the US in the summer of 2016. He knew her from school – she was in the year below him, but was part of his friendship group and apparently had liked him for a while. When we were on holiday, Mac used to creep off to his bedroom every night before dinner. It turned out that he was talking to Amy every single night. It was clear that they liked each other and were already getting on really well. He was very keen to find her the perfect present before we went home, as well as presents for all of her family. He was always very generous – even if it was often with my money!

When we got home, Mac was desperate to go round to see her, so I drove him over to her house about half an hour away from ours. As Amy realised it was him outside, she ran out of her house so quickly that she tripped over their step and fell down – she didn't hurt herself and just laughed. I warmed to her immediately. It was clear that they were perfect for each other – something about them just clicked and I could sense that they did belong together, and very early on could see that they had a future. They just grew closer and closer, and we grew close to her as well. It felt like we finally had the daughter we had always hoped for.

Mac loved to give presents, and would often give away a lot of his own things to people he cared about. It was coming up to Amy's birthday in October. Swee had some lovely rings that she suggested he might like to look through. He did, and chose a sweet little ring with some lovely sparkle. He was so pleased to be able to give it to Amy. They went from strength to strength. It was so nice to see them so happy together.

2016 was working out well.

Chapter 15

US Holidays (Florida)

Some of the best holidays we had as a family were in the US. In 2011, we decided to splash out and take a fortnight's holiday over Easter to Disney World in Orlando. As I mentioned in an earlier chapter, we had taken a short holiday to Euro Disney, but since then we had decided that we would love to visit the genuine US version. It would be Mac's first visit to the US, and his first time on a plane.

We took a fair amount of time looking into the various options. We wanted to get the 'full Disney experience', so knew that we wanted to opt for a Disney hotel. Looking through the range of fantastic hotels, we found the one that appealed to us most: the Animal Kingdom Lodge. As well as all of the usual benefits of a Disney hotel – e.g. access to all of the Disney attractions, free transport around all of the parks – it had live African wildlife in the grounds of the hotel. It sounded fantastic!

The date of the holiday was fast approaching. We had all our clothes, and Mac had his case packed very early. He was so excited! The day came and we made our way to Gatwick Airport. My sister Sandra was kind enough to drop us off. We got to the airport, checked in and made our way to the lounge. At that point I was doing a fair amount of long-haul travel, so I had membership to access the Virgin lounge. That helped to get us in the mood for the trip. Mac was able to play to his heart's content on video games, and Swee and I were able to find somewhere comfortable to relax. Soon enough our flight was called and we made our way to the plane.

We had splashed out on premium economy seats – for me it was a relief to have enough legroom to make the fairly long flight comfortable. Of course, Mac immediately worked out how to work the TV and access the films, so he was set. However, he had never flown before, and so was very excited by the take-off. We had explained what it would be like, and that his ears might pop. We had also told him to look out of the windows so that he could see the ground below as we got higher and higher. As we took off, Mac's eyes opened wide. He told me later how much he had loved the feeling of the accelerating plane as it gained enough speed to take off, and then the feeling once it left the ground. He loved watching the houses getting smaller and smaller as the plane pitched right and left before we finally evened out at our cruising altitude above the clouds. I had forgotten what an exciting experience your first flight could be. Mac absolutely loved every minute of it. It was even enough to draw him away from the TV screen.

The flight was fairly uneventful. It was a daytime flight, but I remember managing to get some sleep, especially as we had comfortable seats. The flight was about nine hours. Eventually we were descending towards Orlando International Airport. Again, we pointed out to Mac the ground getting nearer, and the noises of the landing gear engaging as we came in to land. More firsts, and more excitement for him.

We quickly made it through passport control and picked up our bags. Everything was a first for Mac, from seeing the armed US police like he'd seen on the TV, to picking up our cases from the carousel. He was great at spotting our cases and getting them off – he treated it like a game. We then followed the signs and made our way to the Disney bus for the transfer to our hotel.

The thing that struck me, even in the airport, was the heat and humidity. We had come from a fairly cool mid April in the UK to a normal warm and muggy Orlando. We found the place to wait for our bus, and I remember Swee saying to the woman on the desk, "It's warm today!" (Remember that we were still inside the air-conditioned airport, but it was still warm for us.)

The woman looked slightly puzzled. "Wait until you get outside!"

With that, the bus arrived and we went towards the automatic doors. They opened…and the wall of heat hit us! I'm sure it must have been the hottest weather that Mac had ever encountered. To be honest it was only about thirty-two degrees Celsius, but with high humidity, and it was a big change from a cool April in rural Hampshire. We gratefully got onto the air-conditioned bus and were on our way. We had fantastic seats right at the front and were able to chat to the driver. As we travelled from the airport we engaged him in conversation. He was so friendly, and happy to talk us through some of the aspects of Disney World. As we entered through the gates he explained that the Disney World resort occupied an area greater than Manchester. I hadn't realised the extent of it. There are numerous hotels, four theme parks (Magic Kingdom, EPCOT, Animal Kingdom and Hollywood Studios), two water parks

(Blizzard Beach and Typhoon Lagoon), and Downtown Disney, a whole area dedicated to shopping and restaurants.

After stopping at a number of other hotels on the way, we finally arrived at our hotel. We walked into the stunning lobby, thankful for the air con, and went to check in. The staff were so friendly, asking if we'd ever been before and warmly welcoming us. By now we were tired – it had been an early start back in the UK, and a long journey. We were looking forward to getting to our room.

Animal Kingdom Lodge

The hotel was amazing: the African theme was carried all through the decor. Many of the staff were also from Africa, and their name badges stated which country they were from. After a bit of a false start, getting lost and going in the wrong direction, we finally found our room. We were ready to flop onto our beds, but thought we would have a quick look at the balcony. We went out, and there were a couple of giraffes wandering around and drinking from the water pool! It was extraordinary. You have to give it to Disney – they do Africa so well! We rang room service, had something to eat and drink, turned on the TV (Mac was in seventh heaven with the opportunity to watch twenty-four-hour Disney Channel, given half a chance!), and very quickly crawled into our beds and fell asleep.

There were animals all around the grounds of the hotel, and plenty of viewing places where you could watch them. But to be honest, we had such an amazing view from our balcony that we didn't tend to go elsewhere. There were three savannahs – we overlooked the Sunset Savannah, which meant that at different times of day we could see all sorts of other wildlife as well as the giraffes. We saw

Ankole cattle, cranes, storks, impala and Thomson's gazelles. We were very lucky. One day we took a trip on a jeep to see all the hotel savannahs. It was incredible to see all of the animals close up, watch them being fed, and get some idea of how the place worked. What was clear was how well looked after the animals were.

As well as the animals, the hotel had a lovely main restaurant which served African cuisine – Swee and Mac loved the spicy butternut squash soup. It was self-service, so Mac enjoyed having the freedom to go and help himself once he became more confident. There was a great carvery – perfect for me and Mac as unreformed carnivores. There was also a more informal canteen where you could get takeaway-style food – a favourite for Mac was the proper, crispy southern-fried chicken and Caesar salad. And of course, there were colourful Froot Loops for breakfast.

We were lucky enough to have fifteen full days, so we didn't have to rush. We soon found out that the best approach was to go out early in the morning, and if we did loads, we were ready to come back around lunchtime and spend some time by the pool. The pool was easily the best hotel pool I have ever seen. It was huge, and made to look natural. But most important was that there were plenty of tables around the pool and the bar, and these were shaded. So, even in the heat of the day, it was possible to sit out and not be burned to a crisp. Mac and Swee particularly loved spending time in the pool, swimming away. I was still studying for my ordination and had some essays to complete over the Easter break, so I would happily set up at a table with my books and my laptop, while Swee and Mac splashed away, enjoying themselves in the pool. It was so relaxing.

We discovered early on that you could purchase a big Disney cup. If you did that, you had the right to unlimited drinks from the soda fountain. Mac couldn't believe his luck (and actually, I was pretty chuffed too). He was stunned by the range of different drinks on offer and the huge variety of flavours there were even of the familiar brand that he was used to. His favourite thing to do was to make 'cocktails'. He would mix various flavours and bring them over for me to guess what was in the blend. He was actually pretty good at mixing some tasty drinks, although we soon agreed that root beer didn't belong in any drink! We also met a lovely family with whom we got on well. They had two boys around Mac's age. We spent many of the evenings together, watching as the boys charged around. The hotel was really safe, and we were happy to let Mac come and go as long as he checked in with us frequently and told us where he was going.

It only went wrong on one day. It was late afternoon and we were sitting at our usual table. Mac went off to get changed. For some reason he had misheard us and thought that we were going to meet at the room (actually, we'd agreed that we would meet him back at the pool). We were starting to get worried as Mac had not turned up, and he didn't normally stay away from us for long. After about half an hour, getting pretty worried by now, I got up to go and find him when suddenly he turned up, sobbing, and flung himself into Swee's arms. Once he had realised that we were not coming back to the room, he had gone all round the hotel to find us, getting more and more upset and worried, and finally come back to where we were – we hadn't moved an inch. He was so upset! Even after two and a half years with us, his fear of being left was still with him. After lots of hugs and a couple of soda-fountain cocktails he calmed down. He did still enjoy going round the hotel by himself after that, but he checked more carefully where and when we were going to reunite. He never lost us again.

The Disney parks

Of course, as well as the hotel, we had access to all of the Disney parks. On the first day, the three of us went to Magic Kingdom. Staying in the Disney hotels gives you early access to the parks. As we were still jet-lagged, that worked perfectly for us, so we got on the first transfer bus and made our way.

As I've mentioned before, Swee and I are not keen on scary rides, whereas Mac loves them. He was more than happy to go on by himself, but we felt we ought to go on at least one ride together as a family. As we approached Splash Mountain, we thought that it didn't look too bad – after all, it was all in water and log rafts, so couldn't be that bad, surely? We watched for a little while and noticed that as people splashed down they were all laughing, so we decided to have a go. It was still early, so there was no one in the queue and we were able to go straight on: Mac and Swee in the front of the raft, and me behind. As I am on the heavy side (classic British understatement!) I do worry about these rides, but as we were in the US I was sure we would be fine – and the attendant wasn't at all fazed by our appearance, so all was set.

As you go around Splash Mountain, you go through inside parts populated by characters from *Song of the South*, like Brer Rabbit. They were all singing a laughing song. Then as we came out of that room, the raft started to climb, ready to splash down. Slowly we began to ascend…when suddenly the raft just stopped! There was a grinding sound as it tried to continue upwards. That's it,

I thought, we've broken the ride. We were sitting in the raft at a very steep angle. I had visions of firemen having to come and rescue us. I could see the headlines: 'Fat English tourists break famous Disney ride!' Of course, this was all part of the ride, and after what felt like an age we were going again, over the ridge and splashing down into the water. The sense of relief was so huge that we started laughing – and I realised why all of the people had been laughing when we'd watched earlier.

We had a fantastic time in Magic Kingdom, with Mac trying out lots of the rides. Again he loved It's a Small World, with that tune running through our heads for the rest of the day. He loved Big Thunder Mountain so much he went on it three times on the trot.

We had really enjoyed Magic Kingdom, so Mac and I decided to come back on another day. We got there early, in time to see the opening ceremony. At the opening of the park, the train comes round to the front, and then the Mayor, Mickey and various other characters come round. A family is chosen to ride with them for their special day. There is singing and it is completely magical – I have to say I'm an old softie, and I did shed a tear. (Mac was suitably embarrassed!)

There was one other ride of note in Animal Kingdom – it was a water ride. Mac went on it by himself and I went to the end of the ride to meet him as he came off. The ride consisted of round rafts with six seats. I noticed as I saw people coming off that, in each group, one person was always much wetter than anyone else. You've guessed it: as Mac came off with his party, he was soaked to the skin! He was so wet that I needed to dry him off. Just nearby was a stall selling commemorative towels and T-shirts – I bought one of each for Mac and dried him off. Disney certainly know what they're doing. The woman on the stall just smiled and was able to tell Mac exactly which seat he'd been sitting in – that was the one that always got soaked!

The other place we enjoyed going to was Downtown Disney. This consisted of restaurants and shops. If you wanted anything Disney, that was the place to go. You could ask to have your shopping delivered to your room. We loved our time there, particularly enjoying a jungle-themed restaurant. There was also a traditional ice-cream parlour – Mac had an enormous Knickerbocker Glory. I'm sure he was starting to feel sick, but he was determined to finish it.

As I'd told him before, Mickey Mouse was special and magic. When we were shopping, I took the opportunity to buy a Mickey plush toy and have it sent to the room as a surprise. Mac was so chuffed when it arrived later that day. Mickey is still a much-valued friend.

Other Florida highlights

On the way to the resort in the bus, the driver had mentioned how prolific alligators were in his state, pointing out that there was likely to be an alligator in any body of standing water. We would mention this to Mac, mainly just to pretend-scare him, not really thinking much of it. One evening we decided to have a barbecue with the family we had met. They had a car, so they had gone shopping to get all of the ingredients. We made our way to a set of barbecues that were available on the hotel site for use by residents. It was a fun evening spent cooking and playing games. We were near a large body of water, and we reminded Mac of what the bus driver had said. Later on, he went off for a walk around the lake with his friends and their dad. Despite this, I could see that he was nervous. We thought it was funny, until we saw the small signs by the water, warning of the potential danger of alligators – we stayed right away from that water for the rest of the evening!

As well as Disney we had paid for two other experiences as part of our holiday. The first was a visit to the Wizarding World of Harry Potter in Universal Studios. Swee was not bothered about going, so Mac and I got up early one morning and grabbed a cab to Universal. The ticket included early entrance and breakfast in The Three Broomsticks before looking around the rest of the imaginary Hogsmeade. The recreation was so well done: a fantastic village all overlooked by Hogwarts. It was a little incongruous as Hogsmeade was made out to look snowy, as it usually did in the films, and we were all wandering around in shorts and T-shirts; the temperature already about twenty-two degrees even this early in the morning. As well as breakfast there were rides and plenty of things to see: lots of sweets in Honeydukes, and Ollivanders wand shop. You could get the full experience if you were willing to queue up and wait. We went in with a group of people. Ollivander then picked one of the visitors and she got the full wand-choosing experience. It was great fun, even if Ollivander's English accent came straight from the Dick Van Dyke school of accents. We then went through to the main shop to choose and buy our own wands.

Possibly the main highlight in a holiday of highlights was the visit to Discovery Cove to swim with dolphins. This had been a bucket list item for Swee for as long as she could remember. We headed over to the resort, not really knowing what to expect. As Orlando is inland, there are no natural beaches. Discovery Cove remedies that shortcoming, giving you a place to spend the day swimming and spending time on beaches to your heart's content. There is a lazy river to float around – an absolute favourite of ours – as well as the opportunity to swim with tropical fish in beautiful coves. But the main attraction is the chance to swim with a dolphin. The experience did not disappoint. After getting our wetsuit tops and receiving the safety briefing, we walked through the water to our spot. Then we saw him – Capricorn. He was a huge dolphin approaching us. There were loads of dolphins in the resort, and what is great to see is that if they don't want to come and be sociable, they can just swim away and another dolphin is summoned over. There was no problem with Capricorn – he was so pleased to come and socialise. We went over for our time with him. Lots of photo opportunities (all caught professionally by the staff) as we had a kiss from Capricorn, and then he would take us individually for a swim, pulling us along at a fantastic speed. It was an amazing experience. Capricorn was a brilliant dolphin. He's a bit of a film star, having been one of the dolphins in *Jaws 3* among other films.

It was such a fantastic holiday. It was topped off by winning a beautiful painted ostrich egg in an auction to mark the anniversary of the Animal Kingdom Lodge. There is a great deal of hype about Orlando, but for us it certainly lived up to it. I'd recommend it to anyone.

Chapter 16

US Holidays (New York and North Carolina)

New York

New York is one of my and Swee's favourite cities. I love the place – it is so exciting, with so much that you can do in a long weekend. Sandra had never been to the US, so she was very excited to come with us for a visit to New York in October 2014.

We had booked our favourite hotel, the Marriott Marquis in Times Square. We had a big family room looking over the square – Sandra was closest to the window and overlooked an enormous billboard of Roger Federer advertising some aftershave. It was fun being all in the room together – we laughed a lot.

It is possible to pack a load of stuff into a long weekend. We knew we wouldn't want to walk around for miles – none of us would have enjoyed that – so we booked up to go sightseeing on open-top buses. These took us around the whole of New York, and we were able to get on and off as we liked.

But one of the best ways of seeing New York is by boat. Manhattan is an island, so it is possible to sail all the way round. We took the Circle Line tour that does just that. What a wonderful way to see so many of the sights – and to realise how different parts of the island are, especially as you get to the greener northern end of the island. But of course, it is amazing to sail around the Statue of Liberty, and impossible not to be moved by the spectacle. It always makes me wonder how those immigrants of old felt as they saw that symbol of free America as they approached, looking forward to discovering their own version of the American dream.

We also went to see a Broadway show – a must. I had booked tickets for *On the Town*, the musical original of the famous film starring Frank Sinatra and Gene Kelly. The show was full of great songs and fantastic dancing. We all loved it, especially Mac. On the way back, we passed a shop that sold nothing except baseball caps. Mac was in his element, especially when he saw that it was possible to get one embroidered with your name. He chose a Chicago Bulls cap and had his name emblazoned on it. Needless to say, it never left his head.

But two incidents stick with me.

There is a revolving restaurant at the top of the hotel, on the forty-seventh and forty-eighth floors, called The View. During your meal, you get to see ever-changing views of New York as the restaurant slowly revolves. We had a table right next to one of the windows, and even though it was raining, we were able to see 'the city that never sleeps' in all of her illuminated glory. To go with this, the food was delicious. What Swee hadn't realised was that the whole restaurant didn't revolve; just the outside 'doughnut' – the middle of the restaurant where the desk and cloakrooms are is static. She went off to the toilet. Of course, by the time she came back, the table had moved. Luckily Mac had worked out that she would be confused and had to go and rescue her. A giggling Swee and Mac found us in time for dessert.

The second highlight was towards the end of our time there. Swee and I had had our fill of shopping, but Sandra and Mac wanted to continue, so they went off to the M&M's Store to get some gifts. When they came back a while later, Mac had a huge grin on his face, and Sandra looked a little fraught. While in the shop, harking back to the babysitting incident in the wardrobe, Mac had played his old trick on my sister by disappearing. Of course, she was terrified that she had lost him and didn't know what to do. Suddenly Mac appeared, and Sandra told him how worried she had been.

"You didn't need to worry, Aunty Sandra – I could see you the whole time!"

Luckily, my sister was very forgiving of her nephew.

North Carolina

At the end of year ten at Mac's new school, he had the opportunity to do work experience. We were looking around for something interesting for him to do when Mac mentioned that someone in his class was going to do their work experience in the US. This gave Swee an idea, so we contacted my Aunt Cathy in North Carolina to see if she had any leads. Luckily, good friends of hers owned a chain of traditional US stores called the Mast Stores; somewhat like the general store in *The Waltons*, but selling all sorts of things, especially for tourists. They were very happy for Mac to work there for his work experience. What a fantastic opportunity! We had never had the chance to visit the family there, so we organised it so that we could then tack our summer holidays on the end and make the most of our time. My mum and dad had been to North Carolina a number of times, so they decided to come with us as well. Sadly,

Swee was still suffering with her kidney stone. She had a date for the operation, but until then had decided that it was best for her not to fly in case the stone flared up again. (This turned out to be a sensible decision as she did need to spend some time in hospital while we were away.) Of course, I was unhappy about leaving her behind, but the rest of the family promised to look after her, and she insisted that she didn't want Mac to miss the opportunity.

July came and we were off, flying out to Atlanta. The flight was good and we arrived in good time. I'd recently had a problem with my legs, so wasn't able to walk really long distances, and so had arranged to get wheelchair assistance to get through to the arrivals hall – Atlanta is a huge hub for Delta Air Lines, so the distances to walk are pretty long. My mum also had a wheelchair. When we arrived there were two chairs and only one member of airport staff to push. We were going to have to wait – but, eager to get going, Mac offered to push me. It was hilarious. He was very good at steering me around, making sure I had a couple of near misses with walls and doors, but always making sure I was OK. It was actually good fun as we sailed through passport control and customs. I felt incredibly close to him as he took control, and we laughed and laughed. It was a perfect start to the holiday.

He had been so good on the way through, and I realised how much he was growing up and maturing into a wonderful young man, so I said, "Maybe we should think about getting you that motorbike after all…"

"Really?!"

He looked stunned and so happy. I promised we'd start looking when we got home from our holiday.

Cathy and her husband Dayton live in the Blue Ridge Mountains in North Carolina, in a town called Boone. However, they thought nothing of picking us up from Atlanta and driving us back. We could have stayed with friends of theirs before setting off, but we were all keen to get home, so we set off. Mum and Dad drove with Cathy, and Mac and I went with Dayton. Mac was excited to ride up front so that he could get the best view of everything on the journey.

We had a good journey through Georgia and South Carolina and into North Carolina. It had been hot when we'd arrived in Atlanta, but as we moved further north and climbed into the mountains, the temperature became much more pleasant, and the scenery started to change. On the way, Mac had his first taste of real American fast food. We stopped at a Chick-fil-A, a chicken shop that does the best fried chicken. Mac – and I, come to that – did love fried chicken, and we were particularly taken with the chicken burgers. It was to become a favourite. We arrived in Boone late in the evening. It was so nice to be able to sit out on the deck in the balmy evening, enjoying a drink before we crashed off to bed.

We arrived on the Saturday, which gave Mac a day to get ready for his work experience. To make him feel more comfortable, we drove over to the Mast Store at Valle Crucis, where he was going to be based. It was a beautiful, warm summer's day in the mountains. We sat on the back deck of the store, listening to a traditional local folk music band and drinking our traditional bottles of soda. Mac got to meet a couple of the staff, including a young guy just a bit older than him. They hit it off straight away and had a good chat before we left for lunch. At least we knew Mac would not be so nervous.

So, for the rest of the week, Mac would go off to work early in the morning. Cathy very kindly drove him over every day. She gave him a packed lunch, and they stopped off at Chick-fil-A for breakfast on the way, trying out breakfast burritos or mini chicken sliders. On the first day I went with Cathy to meet him to see how his day had gone. He'd had a blast, helping out with all sorts of chores in the store and meeting and chatting to customers. This tall, handsome young Englishman clearly made a bit of a splash – he soon learned that they all loved the way he talked. I could see how much Mac was enjoying it, and how much he was growing from the experience. First of all he was finding out some of the realities about how long (and occasionally boring) a working day could be. It was also extremely hot in the height of the midday sun at that time of year in the Southern US; even in the mountains. But he also found how interesting it was to make friends in other countries and to compare their lives. And of course, with social media it would be so easy to keep in touch afterwards.

The week quickly came to an end. The store generously gave Mac a large amount of store credit to spend to thank him for all of his hard work. He had his eye on a few things for himself and for friends and family, and quickly found ways to spend it. The manager gave him a glowing write-up for school. All in all, it had been a fantastic experience.

Travelling to and from work, Mac and Cathy had spent a lot of time together. Mac always warmed to people who clearly cared about him and were prepared to give him time. As ever, the car was a great place to chat and to get to know each other. Cathy offered to give Mac the opportunity to drive her car in one of the large car parks nearby – of course, he jumped at the chance. It turned out he was something of a natural. He managed to negotiate the confusion of driving on the other side of the road, and drove really well. Cathy took some videos on her iPhone that showed how much he enjoyed it and concentrated on the task. Later in the holiday, he also got a chance to drive with Dayton in his big pickup.

After Mac's work experience we had planned to go to the beach; to the North Carolina coast. Cathy and Dayton knew a beautiful hotel that they had visited many times before, and we headed over to Atlantis Lodge in Atlantic Beach. It's a fairly long drive, but worth it. The beaches are fantastic and we had the most incredible weather. We had also taken the opportunity to get as much of the American family together as we could, so one of my uncles, David, and his wife Barbara met us there. Sadly, my other uncle, Tom, and Aunt Kathy couldn't be with us. Cathy, David and Tom have ten children between them: my fantastic US cousins. We were so lucky that all but one of them were able to make it and spend time with us. Between them, their families, and all of us, we totally dominated the hotel.

It was the most amazing time. The hotel is right on the beach; just a short walk down the boardwalk. There is also the best pool: it has a waterfall, and is surrounded by oak trees, giving much-needed shade in the heat of the North Carolina day. The rooms are spacious and air-conditioned (a must when it's that hot), and as the hotel is self-catering, there is a small kitchen in each one. All of the family had hotel rooms as close together as possible, but by the evening of each day we would gather on the outdoor sofas in the centre of the hotel complex, making use of the shade and the fresh air as the day started to cool down and light sea breezes began to move the warm afternoon air. We had a week of pretty much wall-to-wall sunshine.

The most enjoyable thing for Mac was that, with so many of my cousins around, most of whom had young children, there was always someone to spend some time with in either the sea or the pool. Mac loved it, and they all loved him. He had fantastic times playing with the younger children or, when they all got a little tired, snuggling up on the sofas outside to play a game or watch a film on his smartphone.

One afternoon, as usual, most of the family were at the pool, taking the opportunity to cool off. Most of the kids had come in from the pool, but one of the boys, Cole, was still in there. Suddenly, as can so easily happen, he got into trouble. Mac happened to be close by and saw, and he jumped into the pool, swam over, and pulled Cole out in one go. Cole was absolutely fine, if a little shell-shocked, as was everyone. Mac just took it in his stride – and it was good to see that his rookie lifeguard training had served him very well.

There are a couple of highlights that I most remember from our time at the beach.

We did a lot of our own cooking, as there were so many of us and we were able to get together in the centre of the hotel. There were lots of grills there, and we decided to have a barbecue – luckily my cousin Adam is a fantastic professional chef. Mac went with Cathy to the supermarket to get the ingredients: plenty of burgers, steaks and hot dogs – loads of meat. While he was shopping, he also decided to buy the ingredients to do some baking. He had become particularly good at shortbread. So, one morning, mixing purely from memory since he didn't have the recipe with him, he made some wonderful shortbread for all the family. I have to admit, it was very good. He managed to endear himself to them even more!

My Uncle Dayton loves to fish. For him, when he had a very stressful job as an attorney in a large university, fishing was one of his main ways to relax. A huge amount of the packing that we'd had to do when we were leaving Boone for the beach was all of his fishing gear. Mac had never been fishing, but loved spending time with Dayton and some of my male cousins who also loved to fish. They would get up very early in the morning and stand on the beach, casting into the sea. Mac loved it, and some of my favourite photos are of him standing on the shore, looking out to sea, fishing. He really enjoyed it, and was very excited when, on his first time, he caught a fish – the photo of him looking so proud as he held up the fish is priceless. One day, Dayton came over early in the morning and told us that he had chartered a small boat to take Mac out sea fishing. Mac couldn't believe it. He, Dayton, and three others went out and spent the afternoon on this boat. They were out there for hours. They came back when it was dark, tanned and tired, having treated themselves to dinner on the way back.

Mac became so close to all of his US family on that trip. They loved his willingness to get stuck into things, and the fact that he was polite and loved all of the experiences that they threw his way. You can see from the photos of us all gathered together how much fun we had. Mac enjoyed the freedom to spend time with various members of the family. I remember most how I would be sitting on the sofas that we gathered on and suddenly I would feel a big pair of arms hugging me from behind, letting me know he was back. My family are spread around the US: North Carolina, Florida, Texas and California. They all agreed that when Mac had finished school, he should come over for six months or so and spend some time travelling across the country to see them all. What a perfect experience that would be, and with loads of family to look after him, spoil him and spend time with him. We also decided that we would come back next year, when Swee was better and after Mac had finished his GCSEs, so that we could show Swee all of the places we had been.

The US just suited Mac somehow – I think he liked the attitude and the outdoor nature of so much of it. I'm sure that's why our US holidays were so special and have made such amazing memories.

Chapter 17

Uganda and Turning Sixteen

The year 2016 was a significant year for Mac. Of course, there was his sixteenth birthday and the run-up to it (more of that later). I have already covered some of the significant events of that year – settling into his new school; making friends and meeting his girlfriend, Amy; our holiday to North Carolina – but describing Mac's run-up to sixteen wouldn't be complete without talking about his trip to Uganda.

Uganda

Our diocese has a link with the diocese of Mityana in Uganda. Over many years the local church has built strong connections with the area, and many of our villagers have visited and helped with various projects, such as building wells and new school buildings. We have also welcomed visitors from Uganda to the village. It has been a very fruitful exercise: we have learned from each other. Our local primary school is connected with a primary school there, and some of the teachers have visited and welcomed colleagues back. Over the years, many of our teenagers have been lucky enough to visit as well.

It is organised through the church, but most of the teenagers are not regular churchgoers. But the trip does help them to build greater bonds with their peers in the village and learn first-hand about another country and how people live there. It helps them realise how much we have in the West, and how different their lives might be in a different country.

It came to the time when Mac's group had the opportunity to go, and Mac was very keen to do it. The agreement was that parents would pay a third of the cost, the individual would raise a third for themselves (e.g. through personal fundraising, or maybe asking for money for Christmas instead of presents), and a third would be raised by the group working together. This meant we spent a year together as a group, raising money to go towards the trip.

Mac raised money from relatives and made lots of cakes and biscuits to sell – with generous relatives, he didn't find it too hard to raise the money for his third. There were plenty of group activities that helped to raise the rest of the money, and Mac was always happy to throw himself into the challenge. One of the most lucrative activities was packing bags at the local Waitrose. Waitrose would allocate three days throughout the year when the group could go along and offer to pack bags, and the customers would then be asked for a small donation. The group were great – they had special Mityana T-shirts and hoodies, so they looked very smart. And they always worked hard and were really polite – it was a fantastic money-spinner. Another successful activity was cleaning out wheelie bins. Most of the group had a Monday off school for staff training. This was also bin day, so all of the wheelie bins had been emptied and were already out on the road. The kids would go round and ask neighbours if they could clean out their bins for a donation. Mac got very involved with our pressure washer (he had done our bins a few times before). They all got very wet, but the village ended up with beautiful, clean and sweet-smelling bins. Some of the parents also got together to lay on a curry night with the kids as waiters and waitresses. Swee and I offered to cook her dad's famous potato and lentil curry to add to the chicken curries and the vegetable curries that were already planned. It was a beautiful warm evening, and the food went down really well. As ever, the kids worked very hard and lots of money was raised.

So, everyone had managed to raise the money necessary for their trip and the date was fast approaching. As well as taking some money for projects over with them, the group would take gifts to give away – nice wash kits, colouring books and crayons for the younger children they would meet – and they prepared some stories and lessons that they would teach in some of the schools. There was so much stuff to take, so packing was a grand logistical exercise, with many of the cases taken up with small gifts and necessities to give away.

Finally, the day in February came. From past experience, the group would leave the village together, with us saying goodbye to our children there rather than all of the parents going along to the airport (and probably making embarrassing nuisances of ourselves as we waved them off for two weeks!). The group were not allowed to take their phones – and to be honest, they wouldn't be of much use in any case as lots of the places they would visit had little if any good mobile signal. For many of them, the screen deprivation was definitely going to be the hardest thing. They all got into the various cars, we waved them off, and then they were gone.

It's amazing how empty a house can feel. It's silly in so many ways, as Mac was often out of the house – whether at school, with his friends, or just messing about on his bike – but something feels different when you know they're not coming back in a few hours; when you know they're away. It's not just the quiet – somehow, the house feels different; less alive.

Meanwhile, in Uganda, Mac was having the time of his life and having experiences not many fifteen-year-olds are lucky enough to have. During the group's time there they helped in a local primary school, spent a day at the secondary school with their buddies (someone of a similar age for them to get to know), visited an orphanage for disabled children, and loads more. They worked on projects, painting and building. Every night they would gather together to discuss and reflect on the day.

One of the things Mac told me he missed most was music as they did not have their phones or any other electronic equipment. But they managed to fill this gap by singing together in the minibus when they were driving to the various schools, and by making their own music. One thing they were allowed was a camera. They all came back with the most amazing pictures – pictures of the schools and the children, pictures of their buddies, pictures of the stunning countryside. They had pictures of them teaching the younger children in school, playing football and other games with some of them, and pictures of them travelling along the long, dusty red roads.

The second half of the trip was an opportunity to go on safari in northern Uganda. After all of the work the group had done, it was a chance for them to kick back a little and to get the experience of seeing some African animals in their natural habitat. Mac had always enjoyed taking photographs and was actually rather good – I can honestly say that some of his safari pictures are incredible. They saw giraffe, antelope, hippos, elephants, lions, rhinos, and all sorts of birdlife. They also visited a chimp sanctuary, although Mac did tell me that he found that quite scary as the older chimps were very loud and pretty aggressive. The babies, on the other hand, were very cute.

Then, at the end of February, my dad and I went to Heathrow to pick him up. I couldn't wait to see him and to hear about all of his adventures. We'd had group emails sent to us to assure us that the kids were OK, but no direct contact. We waited – I could see from my app that the plane had landed – and then suddenly they were there.

The surge of parental love for my boy was huge – and he looked so different. Of course, he had lost some weight as the food had not been his usual fare, but he had grown in stature. Even though he was tired from the trip and the flight, he stood taller, more confident and more self-assured. In short, he had grown up enormously. He had come back as a young man – and with the experiences of a lifetime. The group all looked different, and you could see how much they had shared; how much they had grown together. I knew at that moment not only that Mac had grown, but that he had made some real friends for life.

Turning sixteen

Of course, Mac was very excited to be turning sixteen. I had relented and agreed that he could have a motorbike. Mac was really good on the road: he spent a lot of time on his bike and had gained some good road sense. In any case, he knew he would have to take the proficiency test before he could ride his motorbike. He was also keen to have a little more independence, so that he could potentially ride to school sometimes, or over to Amy's house.

As soon as we got back from North Carolina, Mac and I started looking around for a bike. Actually, there were not loads to choose from. We had discussed and decided that he didn't want a moped style – although they were quite cool, his heart was set on a motorbike that looked like a motorbike. We found a garage nearby that had a good range of bikes, and we saw the one he wanted. It came in black, red or blue. The one in the showroom was black, and Mac was quite tempted. But he decided he wanted the bright metallic blue model. So we ordered it, and organised for it to come in time for his birthday. We also chose a helmet, boots, gloves and a jacket. He was set. Mac was always very grateful for the things he was given, but this time he had a different look about him – he was so excited. I think that because for so long I had said that he couldn't have a motorbike, even when I had changed my mind, he didn't dare believe that it was actually going to happen. When we got home, he rushed in to tell Swee all about his new bike and how lovely it was going to be. I got on and sorted out his insurance and booked his lesson and test so that he would be able to start riding his bike. I had hoped that he would be able to do the test on his birthday, but the nearest we could get was the day after.

A week or so before his birthday, Mac's bike arrived. I have to say I am no motorbike aficionado, but the bike did look great and the colour choice was perfect for him. He sat on it, and I can honestly say it was one of the times I had seen him look happiest.

August 17, and Mac's birthday came along. The family got together to celebrate with him. We celebrated with lots of Kentucky

Fried Chicken – always a family favourite. But really Mac was just impatient to be able to ride his bike. The next day, I had to go to work, but my dad took Mac to the test centre. There they would teach him what was necessary to give him the confidence and ability to ride safely on the road. Then there would be a test at the end to ensure that he was competent to be allowed on the road (the final test to allow him to remove his L-plates would come later). My dad picked him up afterwards and the instructor came to see Dad specially to let him know that Mac had been exemplary. He had easily been the best in the class, and had shown real skill and ability. Mac was beaming. And with that, he became a road user and excitedly got to know his bike.

Of course, one of the key reasons for him to have a bike was to enable him to ride over to see Amy, and to school sometimes. The normal route to the former would have involved driving on a very busy part of the A34; something that neither he nor I was very keen on. So we went out in the car and planned a back route to Amy's house. We made sure he knew the route, and the next day he rode over to her house. Swee and I were so nervous – it was a good forty-minute ride as a 50cc motorbike is limited to thirty miles per hour. We waited for the phone call that we insisted on, and were very relieved when it finally came.

When Mac started back at school in September, he applied for a parking space. Although he knew he would normally get the bus (after all, he had charmed the bus driver to stop outside our house in the morning, giving him a crucial extra five minutes in bed), he was pleased to have the option to ride in. At this stage he still wasn't riding when it was dark, so it would become more restrictive in the winter, but the options were there.

Mac enjoyed his bike so much. His scooters and his bicycles had always represented a degree of freedom that he craved. With his motorbike came a completely different level of freedom. He no longer had to rely on us to take him anywhere, and he didn't need to rely on the school bus either. Of course, he did need to do a few more chores and jobs to earn more money for petrol, but he didn't mind that as a means to an end. He was very happy.

He had changed so much in the past year. All of his problems at school were behind him. He was very happy with Amy, and they had the best time together: they were so comfortable with each other and laughed a lot – a great sign for any relationship. He was talking to his birth family and managing to balance his loyalties to us and to them. He was truly growing into adulthood and becoming a well-balanced, mature and gorgeous young man. He was so much more comfortable in his skin; so much more at ease with himself. He was such good company and it was always a pleasure to be with him. We had spent a great deal of time finding Mac, stripping off the layers and building up the missing pieces. Now we had finally found the Mac who was happy with himself. He had found himself.

Chapter 18

14 October 2016

There are days and dates that become pivotal moments in your life. Days that for various reasons become ones that you will never forget; when your life changes completely in a heartbeat. Often these days are unexpected and you have no way of preparing for them. When you wake up in the morning, you have no idea how differently the day will end from the way you had planned. 14 October 2016 was one of those days for us.

The day started very normally. I often worked from home on a Friday. It gave me a much-needed lie-in compared to the unearthly hour I normally got up to make my way from Hampshire to London for work. Normally as I started to get myself ready for the day, I would be shouting out to Mac to wake up. He had developed a knack for getting up about fifteen minutes before he needed to be outside to catch his bus. This behaviour was so far out of my comfort zone. I come from a family that is always early. When I was a child, we often went on holiday in the South of France, taking the ferry and then driving all the way to the Côte d'Azur. It was a drive we knew well. We had wonderful holidays there. To make sure we would be there in time, we always left early for the journey back to the ferry from Normandy – normally so early that we would catch the ferry the day before the one we had booked! We were nearly always home a day early. So you can imagine how uncomfortable it made me feel that Mac was so happy to leave things until the very last minute to catch his school bus.

However, this Friday was different. Mac had decided he would like to take his motorbike to school so that he could go round to Amy's house afterwards. He was beginning to do this on Fridays – I think he liked to have something outside of schoolwork and preparing for exams to look forward to at the start of his weekend. And where his motorbike was concerned, my love of preparation and setting out early had had an effect on Mac. If he was riding to school, he liked to leave himself plenty of time for the journey.

When I woke up that Friday, I could hear Mac downstairs, making himself some toast and a cup of tea. When he heard me stirring, he came bounding up the stairs and into our bedroom, clearly excited about getting on his bike and showing it off to his friends at school, and then spending some time with Amy over the weekend. He sat on the edge of the bed as I started to get ready and clean my teeth, chatting away to me and Swee.

It was a little before seven, and he was ready to go. It was just starting to get light, so Swee suggested he wait ten minutes or so until the sun was up properly before he left. Mac agreed, then gave me a huge hug and told me he loved me. He was in such a good mood – he loved to ride his bike and having the freedom to go places on his own. He shot downstairs to get his motorbike gear on. He loved his jacket, rightly thinking he looked good in it. We had been looking together at a new leather one he might like to get for Christmas – he was becoming a real lover of nice clothes. He had grown tall and lean and looked good in anything.

It was light now and Mac went down to the garage to get his bike. Our bedroom looks out over our drive, and Swee hung out of the window to wave goodbye. He waved back and drove out onto the quiet village road, indicating as he went (he loved all of the gadgets on his bike!).

It was still quite early so I pottered around, not in any rush to get ready, chatting away to Swee about nothing in particular, just starting to get dressed to go and make some breakfast and let the dog out.

There was a knock at the door. I hung my head out of the window to see who was there. It was a policeman. I was a bit puzzled at first and then my mind started racing, wondering if Mac had got himself in some sort of trouble that had just come to light. So I rushed downstairs and let the policeman in. As I opened the door the policeman checked who I was and asked to come in. He explained that Mac had been in an accident, and that he had come to take me to the hospital and I would need to be quick.

My heart started beating very fast. "Is it bad?" I asked.

He nodded and said again that I needed to get to the hospital as quickly as possible.

"Is he dying?"

He looked at me and just reiterated that things didn't look good. I rushed upstairs to tell Swee. I remember feeling sick and shaking violently. She looked as shocked as I felt, and agreed that I should get to the hospital without her. I told her that she needed to get ready and that I would call Sandra to come and get her (Swee was recuperating from her kidney stone operation, so was not very mobile). I rang Sandra to tell her what had happened and that she should come quickly.

I rushed back downstairs. The policeman was facing the wall in our kitchen, talking on his radio. As I got to the kitchen, he turned around and asked me to sit down. And that was the moment. That was the moment that he told me that Mac had died from his injuries.

The policeman came upstairs with me and I told Swee that Mac had died. She cried out in pain – the visceral pain of any mother losing her child. We just sat crying for a short while, but the overwhelming feeling was shock and disbelief.

Very quickly, we started focusing on the practicalities. The police were keen that Amy did not find out via social media, and so made sure that they got hold of her parents. The police contacted school, and I contacted the headteacher to let her know what had happened. Mac was supposed to be meeting Amy at school and she texted me to say he was late and that she was worried. I didn't reply, but contacted the school again to let them know so that one of the teachers could collect her and protect her from any gossip, before her parents arrived. I also rang Mac's old secondary school, as I knew that so many of his friends and acquaintances were there and I was sure the teachers would want to manage the news. I called work, too, and spoke to one of my managers, but by this time I was finding it difficult to know what to say, and people were so shocked by the news that they found it hard to take in as well.

Swee said she needed to see our vicar, Craig. If she didn't see him and speak to him, she wasn't sure she would walk into the church again. I called him – and he was with us within minutes. By now my sister had arrived, and my dad. My nephews also soon arrived. I called my best friend, Adam. He was also working from home – he lives in Nottingham, but he too dropped everything and made his way down to see us.

The police had managed to get to school to make sure Amy found out from her parents and teachers. They had also contacted Mac's birth mother, and went round to give her the news along with social services. The idea was that contact should be made through social services, but Mac's birth mother sent me a message through Facebook, asking if it could really be true.

"Just call her," Swee said.

So, I asked for her mobile number and called. I spoke to her partner and confirmed what had happened, and again heard the cry of another bereaved mother. I promised to make sure that they were kept informed on what was happening.

Before the police left us, we talked about a number of practical things. First of all, someone would need to formally identify Mac's body. I had never seen a dead body. My mother and my sister have always talked about how seeing a loved one after they have died is a special moment – an opportunity to say a last goodbye and to see them at rest. I have never felt the need to do that. Sandra said that she wanted to see him and would be happy to identify him. Swee and I discussed it, and Swee, sensible as always, told me that I would regret it if I didn't go and see him. She was still not up to the journey and didn't feel a need to see him, but she knew I needed something more. Of course, she was right. We arranged that Sandra, her husband, Swee's brother and I would go to the hospital in the morning. We would meet the policeman there and he would introduce us to the family liaison officer who would be looking after us from then on.

We also started to piece together what had happened. Mac had not got very far from us – little more than five minutes away. He had been riding along the main road when a white van failed to stop at a junction and ploughed into him. Once ambulances and police had arrived, a huge amount of effort was made to save him, and he was finally declared dead at the hospital about an hour after the accident. But to all intents and purposes he was killed outright and died at the roadside: he never recovered consciousness.

The police also suggested we think about whether we wanted to say anything publicly. There was bound to be interest in the local press and they suggested we should make a statement and find a picture we were happy for them to publish. If we didn't, then they would trawl social media for comments and photos and we would lose control of any message we wanted to send. That seemed sensible, so we put our minds to it. The final press release was straightforward and appeared in all of the local media:

> *Police are now in a position to name the motorcyclist who died following a collision near Whitchurch on Friday.*
>
> *Mac Sutcliffe, aged 16, from the Whitchurch area, died after his motorcycle was in collision with a white Mercedes van at the junction of Harroway and Bloswood Lane.*
>
> *Mac's parents have provided the following message in tribute to their son.*
>
> *'It is with enormous sadness that we announce that our beloved son, Mac Sutcliffe, died in a motorcycle accident on October 14. He was a bright flame and shone so brightly in so many lives. We would like to thank everyone for their*

thoughts, prayers and support. It is appreciated and much needed. May he rest in peace and rise in glory.'

Police are appealing for witnesses.

Thinking of this, I decided to look at the local Facebook pages for our area. As I expected, there was a post saying that the road to Whitchurch was blocked as there had been an accident and they had heard that someone had been killed. There were comments from friends of ours saying that their thoughts were with the family and how awful it was. This was still fairly early in the morning. News had not spread as yet, and most of Mac's friends didn't know as they were in school. I was sitting downstairs with our vicar and wasn't sure what to do.

"Put something on there yourself. Then you can take control," Craig advised.

So, I went onto the thread and said that, very sadly, it was Mac who had been killed. The news was out.

The rest of the weekend remains a haze. It was as if time had slowed down and started moving at a completely new speed. From that moment, everything became a blur, and the timings and the order of things become a little sketchy. Since then, my recollections of what happened have been pieced together from my own memories and from talking to others about what they remember.

We spent much of the day talking and sitting. Adam had arrived. He and Sandra did a good job of screening the numerous visitors we had. People were so kind and brought lots of meals. We didn't need to cook for a week! And somehow, no two visitors cooked us the same meal. We had a wonderfully varied diet. We also had flowers everywhere. So much so that when Adam's sister, Louise, was coming round he suggested that, rather than bring flowers, she could bring us some vases. And of course, she did bring us some beautiful glass ones.

Eventually everyone was gone, except for me, Swee, and Adam, who was staying overnight. Swee had gone to bed and Adam and I stayed up talking. That was it – 14 October 2016 was over.

Chapter 19

The Next Few Weeks

Saturday

To our surprise, we slept well that Friday night. We both woke up in the early hours, and, rather than struggle to go back to sleep, we got up and talked, reminiscing about Mac and starting to think about how we might handle the funeral. This became a pattern for us for a few weeks.

The next morning I went to formally identify Mac's body. Adam stayed behind with Swee. It might be a cliché, but it really is at times like these that you find out who your best friends are. Adam had gone for a walk. When he got back, he jumped onto the bed with Swee and said, "Would you like chucky eggs with soldiers? One or two?" It was a treasured memory for Swee, and just what she needed at that moment. When you are grieving and in shock, it can be easy to forget to eat. That's why gifts of prepared meals are such a good idea, and very welcome.

Meanwhile, I was en route to the hospital. On the way, we passed where Mac had died. That was very hard: a place I drive past every day on the way to the train station suddenly had (and continues to have) a new significance. We drove on to the hospital, chatting away to mask our nervousness and sadness as if it was a normal Saturday-morning drive out in the car.

The police had told us where we could park. The door to use was at the back of the hospital, away from the main entrance, and closer to the hospital mortuary. We saw the police, were introduced to our assigned family liaison officer, and made our way in. We came very quickly to the entrance to the mortuary. The police popped in to check that everything was fine, and then showed us in. The room was comfortable and pleasant, with plenty of chairs. From there you could go round the corner to where the body was laid. I went in and asked if I could go and see Mac first. I didn't know what to expect. I had asked if he looked OK – you imagine all sorts of things, especially if someone has been in a motorcycle accident that was violent enough to kill them. We had been told that he looked fine, but I was still apprehensive. After all, up to now no one who knew him had seen him. No one would have known if he looked particularly different.

I went round the corner, and there he was. My beautiful, handsome, loving, quirky, funny, perfect only son was lying there, covered with a purple cover up to his shoulders, with his eyes closed. He didn't look particularly pale. He didn't look any different. His hair was brushed as he would have styled it himself if he had been able to. He had one small mark on his upper lip. He looked like my Mac – he *was* my Mac – and for the first time I could see why sometimes the dead are described as sleeping. He looked like he was asleep – except that he didn't. I can't say why, but it was clear that his soul, or spirit, or whatever it is that makes us, us, had gone. It was a body.

I sat down next to him and looked long and hard. That was

the joker in me wanting to shout out to the police that this wasn't him, and they'd got it wrong – but I didn't. I told everyone it was fine to come round. I looked around at the room. It was nicely done, but with a couple of things that struck me as odd. Someone had clearly thought it was important for there to be flowers – a nice touch, except they were false flowers and not great examples of the craft. There was also a plastic rose placed on Mac's chest. Again, a nice touch, but fresh flowers would have been so much more uplifting. Having dead, plastic flowers felt very strange, and just left me wondering who had made the decision. Even the flowers here weren't alive.

We sat and stood around Mac for a while. I asked if it was OK to take a picture – I wasn't looking for permission; I just wasn't sure if that was a bit weird. But I thought it was important for Swee to be able to see how he looked if she wanted to.

We went back to the anteroom and spoke with the police so that they could talk us through the next steps. The man driving the van had been questioned. There was now an investigation that would take some time and then a decision would be made as to whether any, and what, charges would be made. We talked through our knowledge of the junction where Mac had died; a notoriously nasty one. Tony, my brother-in-law, had been to the site with my nephew to work out what he thought had happened. He talked it through with the police. There would need to be a post-mortem to establish the cause of death. The inquest would be opened and immediately postponed, awaiting the result of any criminal case. The defendant would have the right to an independent post-mortem, but to save the need for two, it was likely that the coroner would insist that only one was done and the report made available to both interested parties.

This was preferable, but might mean the body wouldn't be released to the undertakers as soon as it otherwise might.

There was no pressure to leave, but it was clear that we would have to. I asked to go and see Mac one more time on my own. I went round the corner and sat next to him. I quietly told him that I loved him and missed him, and said goodbye. A few tears flowed as I made to leave. I think I knew at that point that I was unlikely to go and see the body at the undertakers, so this was it. I turned round and left. It was the last time I saw my son.

Sunday

More meals were arriving, and more cards were piling in through the letter box. Adam and Sandra were still doing a sterling job of screening visitors, although they had now slowed down to a trickle. Most people were happy to drop something off and to let us know that they were thinking about us.

With Sunday came church. Of course, Craig had made sure that my services were covered. I had considered whether I wanted to go to church. Part of me knew that I had to go soon. It's fair to say that I was pretty angry with God, and I had plenty of questions for him that I needed to work through. Strangely enough, I didn't feel like my faith was shaken, but I knew that stepping back into our church was going to be hard. It was a place where we had had many significant, happy experiences with Mac: the place where he had served for me at the altar; the place where we had sung in the choir together. The sooner I did go back, the better. However, at this stage I was still craving some anonymity, not wanting to feel the stares of people who knew that I had just lost my son.

Mum and Dad went to the service in the morning and I decided I would go to the quieter service in the evening. Craig took both services and I know that he preached a fantastic sermon in the morning. It is no exaggeration to say that the village was in mourning for Mac. He had been such a presence there as he was always out and about on his scooter or his bike. He was always shouting hello to people, or serving in the shop, or stopping for a chat. It is thankfully rare for a community like ours to lose members so young and so suddenly, but when it does happen it affects everyone. The village stood still that weekend. I have heard from a number of people that Craig's sermon hit the right note and helped them as they started to come to terms with what had happened.

It was time for Adam to go home. He had been the perfect person to have around. He had brought one significant gift for us. Before he'd left home he'd dug up one of the surviving trees that he and Mac had planted. It was still quite small, and able to be potted up. I asked the vicar, and we decided that it would be planted in the churchyard somewhere near where Mac's grave was to be. It was the perfect place, and it is still growing in our churchyard now.

Adam's mum, Mary, lives in the town nearby. Of course, I have known her for a long time. She is a Roman Catholic and arranged for a Mass to be said for Mac. (It took place a couple of weeks later, and I went along. It was very moving. It was one of a number of Masses that some Roman Catholic friends arranged – such a wonderful sentiment.) She asked if she could come along to a service at our church on that Sunday. It was lovely to see her and husband Frank. They went on ahead to the service. I had told Craig I would be coming. I didn't want to draw attention to myself, so I sat quietly on my own at the back of the Lady chapel. Most people didn't know I was there until it came to the communion and I went up to the altar to receive. The tears flowed quietly during that service and it was a relief to let them go. As the service ended, I stayed in my seat as people were leaving. I saw Craig and then quietly left to go home to Swee.

It's strange, but at the end of those two days, I didn't feel that we had cried as much as you might expect. A lot of the time we laughed and smiled as we remembered things, and we were clearly in many ways still in denial and a state of shock. But as Swee and I sat in our bedroom that night, we realised how red and sore our eyes were – a clear sign that we had been crying a great deal more than we'd realised.

One of the things that I had expected when Mac died was that we would feel him in some way around us. However, at first it didn't feel like that at all. In fact, there was a chill and a complete absence of him for a couple of days. Both Swee and I felt it, and it was disturbing. Then, after a couple of days had passed, the house seemed to warm up and his presence was clearly felt. In fact there were times, whether in dreams or out of the corner of the eye, when it felt like you could almost see him. I don't know what that means. Maybe it was part of how we dealt with the loss, or maybe his spirit needed to deal with his sudden death as well. All I do know is that, even now, there are still times when he feels really close.

The run-up to the funeral

Luckily, most of us don't have to think of the practicalities of burying a child – especially a vibrant sixteen-year-old like Mac. This is where undertakers come into their own. The best of them guide you gently and sensitively through the arrangements that need to be made; arrangements that normally need to be made quickly. If you think of the time that the average wedding takes to arrange, funerals are normally arranged in less than a month.

We knew our undertakers well. They are good friends of my sister and brother-in-law, and we had dealt with them fairly recently, when Swee's parents died the year before. Steve needed some clothes for Mac. I had a look in his bedroom (never an easy thing to do as he was one of the untidiest teenagers I have known). We found a polo shirt I knew he liked, one of his favourite bomber jackets, and a pair of skinny trousers. It was an outfit I knew he would have been happy to wear for a smart occasion. I wanted to find his favourite pair of Converse that I had given him, but it was an impossible task. But I had a pair of shiny brown brogues that I knew would fit, and so handed them over to the undertaker. I knew Mac wouldn't have been keen, but thought they were smart enough to be buried in!

(As an aside, a few months later my nephew's partner went to see a medium. I am pretty sceptical about these things – I tend to think that they are extremely good at reading signs and are then able to narrow down their more general statements. However, there was one thing she said that I share here as I have no good explanation for it. Someone sounding like Mac came along and said all of the usual things about being happy etc. There were some statements that were pretty accurate. But the one that floored me was that he was rolling his eyes and looking at his feet. The medium then said, "He's looking down at his feet and rolling his eyes, and saying, 'Those shoes, Dad!'" No one knew about the shoes except me, Swee, and our undertaker. Vicky, who went to the medium, had never heard the story and didn't know what it meant.)

We also wanted to place some items in Mac's coffin. He had recently ordered some Chocolate Jazzies, which arrived after he had died, so they went in with him. When Mac had first come to us, a family friend had given him a folding silver photo frame with room for a picture of me and a picture of Swee on either side, so that if he went away, he could take it with him. He did take it with him whenever he went on a trip, so we included that. Finally, when I'd gone on my trip to Tokyo, Swee and Mac had bought me a small teddy that we named Tokyo Ted. They put him in my case as a surprise. Then, whenever I went away, I would take Tokyo Ted with me – he was a very well-travelled ted. As Mac started going on trips, he would also take Ted. It was particularly fitting that Tokyo Ted should go on Mac's last journey with him.

One of the difficulties we had to face was how to include Mac's birth family. We knew we needed time to ourselves to grieve, and our priority was us, our family and our close friends. We had no real relationship with his birth family and had only ever met his brothers. All contact was to take place through the police and social services, but increasingly we were being contacted through Facebook and social media by members of the family. We had promised that we would keep in touch about the arrangements, but we also wanted to protect ourselves as we needed some privacy to grieve. Once Mac's body had been released and prepared for viewing, we made sure time was put aside for the birth family if they wanted to go and see the body. We had decided that we did not want them at the burial, but they would be welcome to attend the memorial in the afternoon.

This did not go down well. The birth family had wanted to be fully involved, with Mac's brothers carrying his coffin. It was difficult for us: while I could see their side and felt for them, they had not been fully in Mac's life since he was five years old, and we had seen him through all of his difficult times and helped him to get over the difficult start we'd had. The reality was that there was no easy way to fully accommodate everyone's needs, but as his parents, we knew that we needed some privacy, with those closest to us around us, to grieve the loss of our son. Things became particularly unpleasant on Facebook, with Mac's birth mother and her partner accusing us of all sorts of things and being quite abusive. However, we tried to ignore all of this and prepared packages of Mac's things for various members of his birth family, including giving back to his birth mother the toy lion that she had given to him when he was taken into care, and that he had kept. I don't know if they were grateful – they never let us know. We also suggested that they could come early to the memorial so that they could spend some time alone at the graveside. They did come to the memorial, but left halfway through, accusing me of criticising them during the eulogy – I think the truth is that it was just too difficult for them.

The reactions of Mac's friends

It is so hard for fifteen- and sixteen-year-olds to lose one of their own. In so many ways Mac's friends were looking for ways to mark his death and to do something positive.

Some of his older friends rode their motorbikes together to where he had died. We met them there with Amy and her family. The kids tied ribbons around the signpost that was there, and left flowers. Finally, my brother-in-law, Tony, left a lamp with a candle shining that was there for a few days.

I was keen to be around to talk to any of Mac's friends who wanted to. His Uganda group met fairly regularly and I went along to one of their meetings. It was important to be able to talk about Mac. We brought along pieces of music to discuss, and I was able to take one of the pieces that Mac and I used to sing together and which particularly reminded me of him. (The one I chose on that occasion was '7 Years' by Lukas Graham.)

Mac's school was amazing. They had a whole year and more of students upset and in shock, as well as many of the staff. The students were keen to do something, so the head set aside an area for them to bring in flowers and leave notes. I went to see the tributes and it was incredibly moving. All of the cards were collected together and put into a remembrance book for us, together with many notes from the students and teachers telling us how they felt about Mac. When we went to visit, we were presented with Mac's school picture, which had been taken just a couple of weeks before he died. Mac's school photos were often not good – he normally had an overly cheesy grin in them. But this one was just perfect – it is a beautiful picture of him. The head also told us that they were building a contemplation garden and had decided that there should be a quiet corner with a bench, and that would be named Mac's Corner. I was overcome – he had only spent just over a year in that school, but he had clearly made an impression. I can't praise the school enough for their approach and their support for us and for their students, then and over the many months after that.

The funeral and memorial had been set for 5 November. I offered to speak to some of Mac's friends about it, as I was sure that most of them would not have been to a service like this and I didn't want them to feel uncomfortable or not know what to do. I spent a lunchtime chatting away to them, answering their questions and talking them through the structure of the service. I hope it helped them – it certainly helped me.

Chapter 20

5 November 2016

As a priest I have always believed that funerals are a very important stage in the mourning process. I hear many people struggling to think what their loved one would have wanted – would they want fuss, what hymns would they like, what flowers would be best? – and it is important to feel that you have done your best by them. But it is also important to make sure that the funeral serves those who are left behind. It really can be an uplifting event and a chance to celebrate the life of the person we have lost. As a Christian, I also feel that there is a message of hope: that through our sadness we know that there is hope for more for all of us. Whatever your beliefs, I think the funeral is an important rite of passage.

Swee and I started planning Mac's funeral straight away. We found that although we did sleep well even on the first night, we were wide awake in the middle of the night. In those dark hours, rather than struggle to go to sleep, we had long conversations reminiscing and talking about Mac. And we also started to plan what we wanted at the service to really celebrate his life.

We knew that we wanted him buried – the churchyard is so close to our house, and our village had been such an important part of his life that we knew we wanted him laid to rest in the soft earth of our wonderful churchyard. As I mentioned in an earlier chapter, our former vicar, Michael, had died suddenly and was buried in our churchyard. As the active incumbent of our parish, a special place had been found to bury him behind the church. Mac had been so close to him that I secretly wondered if we would be able to put him next to Michael. Our present vicar, Craig, had been with us the whole morning of Mac's death. Then he had gone off in the afternoon, and spoke to me afterwards to say that he had been unable to concentrate on anything, and so had started thinking about Mac's funeral. Before I had a chance to ask, and as he knew that Mac had had such a special bond with Michael, he asked us if we would like to place Mac next to him. How fantastic! It was the perfect place.

We then started to plan the funeral itself. We had to think carefully about how we could find our own space to mourn, while knowing that there would be plenty of others who would want to come and pay their respects – not least his birth family. So, we decided that we would have a funeral in the morning with close family and the families of Mac's godparents, and then an open memorial service in the afternoon.

I had spoken to the partner of Mac's birth mother on the morning he died. But apart from that, the intention was that everything would be done through the police and social services. As I mentioned in the last chapter, it had become difficult with his birth family, but we knew that we needed people around us at the funeral itself who would be there to support us on what was going to be a difficult day. We tried to accommodate the birth family as much as possible, and made it clear that if they came early, they would be able to go to Mac's grave beforehand.

Putting these complications aside, the services came together very quickly. The Bishop of Basingstoke, David Williams, had met Mac on a number of occasions and offered to take the funeral in the morning. The memorial service in the afternoon would be led by Craig, with the other priests in our benefice, Terry and Dodie, leading the prayers. Craig would preach, and I would read the eulogy. It was such a simple decision as to whether to do the eulogy. Although there was a part of me that was worried that I would not be able to deliver it, I wanted to do this as I knew I was the one who could write and deliver the best tribute to Mac – and I owed him that.

So, we started to put the services together. The morning service was to be the more sombre – the chance for those closest to him to support each other in our grief, and to lay him to rest in our churchyard. For this we chose simple hymns and readings.

We wanted the memorial in the afternoon to be more of a celebration. We chose more rousing hymns, and ones that would mean something to those attending: 'When a Knight Won His Spurs' was a hymn that Mac's school friends, their parents, and the primary-school teachers would recognise as a favourite that was often sung at our village school. And we finished with 'I Vow to Thee, My Country' as a hymn that we could all belt out at the end. I always feel that a really good sing at a funeral helps with the huge mix of emotions. At the end of the service we would have some songs from some of the musicals we loved as a family, including 'Popular' and 'For Good' from *Wicked*; the first show we had seen together.

As we were planning the memorial, Swee decided that she wanted to say something. Her great love is poetry, and on the internet she found a poem called 'A Picture of You' that was so fitting it had to be used. The plans were in place.

Then the day finally arrived. It was a cold and sunny November day. When I woke up in the morning, I had a curious mix of emotions. First there was the sadness that had become my new default emotion. It didn't mean that I was constantly melancholy, but the sadness was there whenever I didn't cover it with something else. I was also apprehensive: would the services go well, would I be able to make it through them without 'showing myself up', would Swee be OK, would the services do Mac justice? And then there was a strange sense of excitement. We had planned the services well. I knew the morning was going to be very hard as we finally laid Mac to rest, but there was something of a performance in the afternoon. I was also excited to see who would come, and to hear the stories they had of Mac.

We had arranged for the coffin to come to the church before the service. Craig would then escort Mac in – we knew that we didn't want to follow the coffin in after everyone else had taken their seats. We had decided that we would get to the church early enough (not difficult when you live opposite!) so that we could take our seats and not have to walk down the aisle in front of everyone. The coffin arrived – we watched out of the kitchen window as it was taken into the church. There were beautiful flowers. We had asked for multicoloured flowers to cover the coffin. My sister and her family had bought a beautiful 'M' in purple and blue (Mac's favourite colours), my mum and dad had bought a display of white flowers, and Mac's girlfriend Amy and her family had bought a heart. The coffin was carried into the church.

We left it a little while and then went to go and take our seats. I have to say, I don't remember much about the morning service. I remember the intense emotions and the profound sadness. I can remember seeing the faces of those I love the most who were all in that church with us, looking so sad. There were fifty or so of us: my mum and dad (Swee's parents had died the year before), our siblings and their families, Amy and her family, and then all of Mac's godparents and their families. Mac had ten godparents, so the numbers added up. I can remember hugging a lot of people before and after the service. We also had my Aunt Cathy and cousin Eric from the US. So many of our US family had wanted to come but couldn't, so we were all happy that Cathy and Eric could represent them.

From the service itself, I don't remember much apart from some of the words of Bishop David. David is a remarkable preacher, and he always hits the mark. But I know this was difficult for him. Two remarks from that sermon have stuck with me. First, I remember him speaking directly to Swee, and reminding her that the Virgin Mary too had experienced the loss of her son. Then the remark that stands out most for me was when he said, "Despite dying young, I am sure that Mac lived a full life as he experienced love." (We have engraved on Mac's headstone, 'He lived a full life because he loved and was loved.')

As the service finished, my two nephews stood up with the pall-bearers to take Mac to his final resting place in the gentle earth of our churchyard. Swee and I stood at a little distance – it was too painful to be right next to the grave as we watched the coffin being lowered into the ground.

And with that, the funeral was over. We thanked the bishop and his wife, and went back to our house to have a rest and to get ready for the memorial service in the afternoon. My sister accompanied everyone else to the pub where we had arranged lunch for them.

Then it was time for the memorial. I was robing for this, and went over early to get ready and to start to greet people as they arrived. We were expecting the church to be quite full but weren't sure how many would come. We knew there would be plenty of our friends from the village and lots of Mac's school friends and teachers. We guessed there would be about 200 or so. The church is quite big, so we knew that it could take them.

People started to arrive. Mac's headmistress and some of his teachers arrived early. They had some flowers, and asked if it would be OK to take them to the grave. Then more and more people started to arrive – I recognised most of the faces, but not all of the younger ones. It was clear that an enormous number of Mac's peers had turned up. Each had a look on their face that was a mixture of sadness and disbelief – you don't expect to say goodbye to one of your own when you're fifteen or sixteen. People just kept arriving: more and more people from the village, friends from work, friends of mine who had been ordained with me, and people Swee had worked with in the local GP's surgery.

By now the church was getting very full. Swee and I sat down and started to gather ourselves as we saw the church filling up. Every single gap and available space was filled. The service began with the first hymn, 'In Christ Alone', and the church was filled with the most extraordinary sound.

The service continued, and we eventually got to the point where Swee would read out the poem – the words were so moving and completely appropriate to the situation. We had decided that Swee would not stand up to speak, but would speak through the microphone from her seat. Somehow, she managed to say the words with strength and emotion, but still got through every word. There was a hush in the church punctuated by a lot of quiet weeping. The poem had hit a nerve for everyone in there as it so aptly described what was in Swee's heart.

I then had the unenviable task of following with the eulogy. I got up and walked to the lectern. As I turned around, I saw for the first time just how many people were in the church. It is the fullest I have ever seen the church before or since. The ushers and churchwardens lost count of all, but the estimate was that there were more than 500 people squeezed into our beautiful village church to pay their respects and to celebrate Mac's life. I took a deep breath and launched into the eulogy. As I spoke, I became calm and very close to Mac. I knew that I was doing the very best that I could for him at that time. I managed to get through the whole thing – with my voice cracking on the last couple of words. I returned to my seat, glad that it had gone well, and exhausted.

Two of Mac's classmates who are great musicians then paid tribute to him with a song they had written to express their sadness. Then there were the final set of prayers, the commendation, and the final hymn.

At the end of the service, everyone was invited to gather at Mac's grave to say some final prayers. Swee and I did not join them, but stayed behind in the church. I have seen pictures of everyone gathered in a wide circle around Mac's grave; the winter sun shining as it lowered in the sky. I am told it was the most emotional and moving moment for all who were there.

Finally, most of us retired to the village hall for tea and cake. Mac loved cake and many of the wonderful bakers in the village had baked to make sure that we had plenty for everyone. We had also ensured that there were macaroons – always a favourite for us, not least because it was a nickname for Mac. Swee and I were very tired by now, but it was so wonderful to talk to people, and uplifting to see how many wanted to be there to mark his life. Reading the hundreds of cards that we received, it was astonishing to realise how many people's lives Mac had touched.

Of course, the evening was Bonfire Night. We had invited all of our family round to our house for a takeaway. We didn't want to be on our own, but we certainly didn't want to cook. Our US family were very keen to go and see the bonfire and fireworks being laid on in the village, so they went off with my nephew and his daughters. It was a beautiful clear and cold November night – perfect for Bonfire Night. It was such an appropriate day for Mac's funeral: he loved Bonfire Night and fireworks, and one of the first occasions he had come to the village for was to go to our local display.

Once everyone was back, we ate and talked about how well the day had gone. Soon we were all very tired, and everyone left and Swee and I were on our own again. The day had been extremely sad, but so uplifting too. Seeing so many people gathered in that church to celebrate Mac is something I will never forget.

Swee and I went to bed and had the best sleep we'd had in weeks.

Chapter 21

The First Year

"Getting through the first year is the hardest." That's something you often hear after you have been bereaved. And while it might on one level sound a little trite, there is something about the year of 'firsts': the first Christmas without him, the first birthday without him, the first Mother's Day and Father's Day without him – all culminating in the ultimate first: the first anniversary of his death.

I remember making three definite promises on the day that Mac died.

First was not to be angry. It would have been so easy to be angry at the situation, and a completely natural part of the grieving process. I've already admitted that I was pretty angry with God (mind you, I was pretty sure he could take it, and there are some notable parts of Scripture where the writers are angry with him as well – particularly the Psalms). I could have been angry at other people; particularly the van driver who didn't stop and knocked Mac off his bike, or the passenger in the van who didn't see anything because he was too busy looking at his phone. But I knew being angry wouldn't work for me as I would become consumed by anger that would do me no good at all. I have pretty much kept to that promise.

The second promise was to have no regrets. I can honestly say that this was an easy one to keep. Swee and I agreed early on that we were so pleased that we had never held back from doing the things that we wanted to with Mac when we had the chance. We had been on wonderful holidays and had made the best memories. Now those memories were all we had left, so we thanked God we had done so much and helped Mac to become the best version of himself that he could be. We had given him a lot of things, but again we did not regret this as he had always been grateful and had missed out on so much in his early life. Of course, I could have regretted changing my mind and letting him have a motorbike. I could have regretted letting him ride to school that morning instead of offering to pick him up from Amy's. But I remember so much more the look of surprise on his face when I said he could have a motorbike, and his joy and pride when it arrived. I remember the care he took with it and the excitement he got from the freedom it gave him. I remember how good he was on his bike, and the fact that he was sensible and rode it well. He was killed because a van driver drove carelessly, made a mistake and ploughed into him. Mac did nothing wrong – he was in the wrong place at the wrong time. Why regret all of the happiness and pure joy that his motorbike brought him?

My third promise was not to give up. As Mac was no longer alive, I owed it to him to live my best life. And I confess here that this has been the hardest promise to keep, although it's one I keep working at every day.

Losing a child is hard. Losing a child is painful. Losing a child feels wrong on so many levels. We put our hopes and our futures into our children. We look forward to helping them grow; to seeing them become adults and live the best lives they can. We look forward to taking part in their futures; seeing them settle down, and maybe marry and have children of their own. We look forward to the prospect of being grandparents, especially if we have been lucky enough to have had fantastic grandparents ourselves, hoping to follow their examples with our own grandchildren. With the death of your child, in a moment it as if all your hopes for the future have been snuffed out.

The other thing that happens is that your life comes into stark perspective. All of the times when you worried when bringing up your kid – the mistakes they made; the bad choices – though apparently serious at the time, suddenly are seen for what they were: nothing in the grand scheme of things. You know that you would go through all of those worries again just for one last hug; just to stop the incredible pain that won't go away.

I remember doubting myself. What was my purpose in life now? Why should I bother getting up tomorrow? What should I do with my life? Was I still a dad, even though my only child was dead? If you lose your parents, you become an orphan. If you lose your partner, you become a widow or a widower. But what is a parent whose child had died?

Of course, I still had Swee, and we were lucky that our relationship was very strong. I was confident that this experience would only bring us closer – after all, we were all we had. It's not that we didn't have family and extraordinarily good friends, but in the final analysis, they all had other people in their lives who came first. Now it was down to me and Swee. We had been very happy before Mac came along. Yes, we had been sad that we had not been able to have a family, but we were very happy with our lives more generally.

Somehow, now that Mac had died, we needed to find a way back to the way things were.

But it's not that easy. It's never going to go back to the way things were. For one reason: you have changed. Parenthood changed you first of all, and now bereavement has changed you again. As time moved on, I could feel that I had changed fundamentally; that I was now a different person. I wasn't necessarily unhappy with that; just a little surprised. I needed to try to find out who that new person was. In fact, before I went back to work, I grew a beard – partly because I had become bored of shaving, but also because on an unconscious level I wanted my outward appearance to change to reflect the changes inside.

Looking back, all of these things were the early signs of depression. I knew that was a possibility, but I have always been incredibly positive, normally optimistic, and I have been lucky enough not to have suffered with any mental issues in the past.

After a month, I returned to work at the Financial Conduct Authority. It was a week after the funeral, and I was keen to get back to some form of normality and routine. I always arrived in the office early, normally before any others from my department. I was able to get to my desk pretty much unscathed – in fact, it felt like a relief to be back. My work colleagues had been extremely supportive. A number of my managers had come to the funeral. My senior bosses had sent wonderful personal letters and were generous with time off for me to start to sort things out. So many of them had children of a similar age that I think they couldn't help but put themselves in my shoes and feel some of my horror and pain. I had known many of them for a long time, and they had walked the journey of Mac's adoption with me, so they knew the full story.

The first few days were OK. I had got very good at hiding my true feelings, and telling everyone that I was all right and they weren't to worry. I was doing the job tolerably well, but I knew deep down that I could do so much better. I knew that I wasn't being as supportive of my department as they needed – they were patient with me, but it couldn't go on forever.

After getting through Christmas, it was clear to me that I was going to need more time off – I still needed to work through so much. There were practical things to attend to, like clearing out Mac's remarkably full and untidy bedroom. I needed to spend more time with Swee. I needed to be at home. Again my employers were very supportive and I was signed off sick for a month. It was also agreed that I needed a change of role in the organisation or a secondment to another one – so much had changed that I couldn't keep coming in and doing the same job, at the same desk, with the same people as I had before Mac had died. Luckily we were able to organise a secondment to a sister organisation, and that helped no end.

But on top of all of this, I needed to admit that I was depressed and that I would need some help with that. I was not some superhuman who could do all of this on my own. The pain of losing a child is almost impossible to bear without some form of help, I think. I took that help, and with it I was able to see how much people were mourning with me. I don't mean Swee – she and I would talk all the time about how we felt about Mac. For a while every Friday morning was difficult and dark. But we cried and laughed together all the time, and often when one was down the other would be up and we could help to balance each other out.

What I did start to notice was how the rest of the family were affected. Of course, our siblings, their families, and my parents were all mourning him. My nephew's daughter was much the same age as Mac and she missed him dreadfully. Mac's girlfriend Amy was really struggling, but we were building a relationship with her, sharing our stories of and our love for Mac.

The people who affected me the most were my mum and dad. My dad was eighty-two and my mum had just turned eighty a month before Mac died. We had wonderful pictures of Mac with them at her birthday lunch. But if it is wrong to lose a child, how wrong is it to lose a grandchild? They have since told me that, along with the pain of losing Mac, they also had to bear the pain of seeing their son and daughter-in-law dealing with the huge loss. I know that in the first moment I saw my mum on the day Mac died, I broke down, and she just hugged me. To this day, my dad says hello to Mac every time he drives past the place where he died (which is probably most days), and tells him what they are planning for the day. At times my heart could break for them.

The first few months

One of the difficult things to deal with as time moves on is when you come across someone who doesn't know what has happened. To begin with you get quite used to telling people and then immediately finding yourself trying to put them at ease as they attempt to deal with the shock of the news. As more time passed, I found that I wanted to avoid the conversation if I could – partly because I didn't want to keep repeating what had happened, but also because I wanted to protect these relative strangers from the news.

This did lead to some bizarre decisions. For example, Mac and I always went together to have our hair cut – it was one of those

Saturday-morning father/son events every six weeks or so. We always went to the same barbers and they got to know us – not by name, but well enough to recognise us and have a pleasant conversation. As time passed after Mac died, I just couldn't see how I could go back to that barber's shop. I didn't want to have to have the conversation about Mac, as I was sure they would ask where he was. What do you say? Do you lie and say he is away, or do you tell the truth and tell them he's dead, knowing that that will kill off all conversation and won't be a pleasant thing for them to hear in response to attempted small talk? It might seem strange, but I agonised over what to do so much that I have never returned.

What I did work out pretty quickly was that I wanted to take more control of how I was feeling. It wasn't that I wanted to stop it, but I wanted to make sure I was as prepared as I could be. The main part of that was working out how to deal with the year of 'firsts'. What were the occasions that would be hardest to deal with, and how were we going to prepare for them?

The first anniversary to deal with was 14 November – moving-in day. For the three of us this had always been the day we celebrated. We didn't celebrate the day the adoption was made legal, or the day we went to court to be given the certificate. We celebrated the day Mac moved in – it was the most significant for all of us. As this was only just over a week after Mac's funeral, in the first year we didn't do much at all. Our tradition had been to go to the chippy and snuggle in front of the TV as we had done that first time eight years before. So Swee and I did that quietly and marked the occasion on our own.

The first significant time to deal with was Christmas and the run-up to it. As I have said earlier, we loved Christmas and enjoyed the preparations. Mac and Swee used to love decorating the house, and I used to love getting the food ready; making the puddings and the cake on Stir-Up Sunday. What would we do this year? The last thing I felt like doing was covering the house with decorations and tinsel. So we bought a very small tree in a pot, and put a few decorations around it. We got some of our favourite Christmas ornaments out, and that was about it. It was enough somehow – it would have been miserable to have nothing, but we didn't want it to look the same as it had before. I had agreed with Craig that I would not have to take a Christmas service. I was not in a good place to preach the joy of Christmas to everyone. I also still felt that the focus would be on me and the fact that we had lost Mac, and that was not appropriate. Time still needed to pass.

Christmas Day came and went. As usual, the family gathered at Sandra's house with her sons and their families, Mum and Dad, and Swee's brother Andy. It was one of the first days that Swee had been out. Of course there were tears, especially when we all gathered at the table and Mac wasn't there. Swee and I went through the motions and soon returned home. I thought we did OK, but looking back at pictures now, I can see the pain and anguish in our eyes. It was still so raw, and such early days.

Miles for Mac

Soon after I returned to work, one of the senior directors asked me to come to see him about a personal matter. I had worked with Chris for a number of years, although I had never worked directly for him, so I was a little intrigued. He had written us the most wonderful and personal letter just after Mac died, and had been incredibly supportive. He told me that he had discussed with other senior management the potential response of our organisation to Mac's death, and that he would like, if it were possible, for the Financial Conduct Authority to raise some money for Children in Need in Mac's name. He asked if I had any ideas. We quickly decided that some form of walk would be appropriate. We could then get plenty of people involved and hopefully raise a significant sum for the charity. We thought maybe a sixteen-mile walk would be fitting as Mac had been sixteen when he died. By pure coincidence, I measured the rough distance between Mac's school and our village and it turned out to be almost exactly sixteen miles. It was perfect: the walk could make a 'pilgrimage' between Mac's school and home – the journey that he never got to complete on that day.

Of course, the idea was the easy part. We then needed to go about organising it. I worked with Chris's office to organise much of the logistics back at the FCA. We needed to talk to the police, set up JustGiving pages, gather names of potential walkers, and make sure plenty of people knew about it so that we had lots of support. We decided to do the walk in September as hopefully the weather would be good, but not too hot – perfect for walking a distance through the countryside. We also organised T-shirts for everyone – a great way to spot them on the walk!

Then there was the route itself. Luckily I know a few people who like to walk through our local countryside. They planned out and walked the route, making sure that it was cross-country and avoided the big roads as much as possible. Luckily half of the walk was able to follow a traditional route – the Test Way – so we knew it would be a well-worn and picturesque path. I made sure we had plenty of marshals at points where it might not be obvious which direction to take. We wanted to be sure that we would not lose anyone and that we could get help easily if anyone was in trouble. The walk broke nicely into two halves, with a good place to break for lunch. This also meant that those people who didn't want to walk the full sixteen miles could join at the halfway stage and still take part. Finally – but most importantly – we organised delicious refreshments at the end. When promoting the walk, I'd promised beautiful countryside and really good cake.

The day came. Most of the group met at the end point of the walk. We then bussed them to the start at Mac's school, where we convened in the contemplation garden. This was the garden that had been planned before Mac died, and where the school had decided to put aside a quiet corner for students to be able to sit and gather their thoughts. This was known as Mac's Corner. One of his school friends had raised money for a beautiful bench to remember Mac. Swee and I had bought a yellow metallic sculpture called *Blowing Bubbles* to be placed there as well. The garden was beautiful and was developing well. It had been opened in June by the Bishop of Basingstoke in a ceremony that coincided with the last day after the exams for Mac's year. They all turned up to see the garden and to mark the occasion. It had been a very moving day.

But back to the day of the walk. The weather was glorious! Sunny, no rain, and not too hot – the countryside was at its best. I thanked everyone for coming and started them off. The walk went really well. As well as about thirty or more walkers from the FCA, some of my friends joined in, and some of the villagers. It was such a lovely day to do the walk – I was so grateful that it didn't rain. That would not have been such a nice experience! As the walkers came down the hill that led to the village, the church bells were ringing.

A number of them told me how much that had cheered them on the last lap. It was so nice at the end as everyone gathered together and sat and ate cake, chatting about how much they had enjoyed the day. And to top it off, the walk raised more than £11,000!

Return holiday to North Carolina

As we had had such a great holiday the year before when Swee was not able to come, we had planned straight away to return the year after. Of course, Mac had died just a few months after that holiday, but we still thought it would be a good idea to go, so that Swee could see all of the places where we had been with him.

Sadly, she was unable to go again. Her health had suffered since Mac had died and she was not well enough to travel. However, we decided that I would still go and spend some time with the family. I was reluctant to go without Swee, but my US family were planning a bench and a tree in the grounds of the shop where Mac had worked, so it felt as though I should go. And to be honest, I was looking forward to a change of scene.

I don't mind travelling alone. However, it was weird this time. It was almost exactly a year after the holiday that I had spent with Mac, going to the same places. I hadn't seen many of my family since then, so I knew it would be quite emotional. But I was looking forward to it all the same.

I flew to Atlanta and was met by one of my uncles and aunt. They are from Texas but had been spending some time in Georgia for a holiday, and were happy to come and pick me up and take me up to Boone, as they were also planning to spend some time there. It was so nice to have the time to spend with them, and to chat and catch up.

Soon enough we were in Boone. It was strange as we arrived at my Aunt Cathy's house. It had such strong memories of Mac. It was late, but it was so nice to sit out sipping a bourbon cocktail on the deck in the warm evening. As we did so, Cathy told me about a strange coincidence. The year before, Mac and I had bought her some very large, deep-sounding wind chimes as she loved them so much. They were hanging from a tree in the wooded part of her garden. They had a distinctive, resonant sound, but as they were large they only really rang when there was a sufficient breeze. Cathy told me that soon after Mac had died, she was standing on her deck, thinking about the times she had spent there with him. Suddenly the chimes started to ring – and she swears there wasn't a breath of air. Even now, when they ring she says it reminds her of him and makes him feel closer. Similarly, I have always been told that if you see a robin, it is a loved one coming from heaven to visit. In the US they have the same legend, except the relevant bird is the red cardinal: a beautiful red-coloured bird with striking plumage and a distinctive crest. We saw a fair few when I was there – it's nice to think that in some way Mac was with us.

We had such a relaxing time in Boone. We had also planned to return to the same hotel at the beach. It is such a wonderful place. As there were fewer of us we spent less time in the communal area as we had enough room outside our own rooms. However, on the first night we did go and sit there, as we had done so many times the year before. Sitting there, I felt very close to Mac. It felt as if, if I turned round, I would see him bounding up from swimming or fishing with his cousins, ready to grab me around the shoulders and give me a big hug. Oh, how I missed those hugs!

Music for Mac

Fairly early on after Mac died, I decided that I wanted to do something positive to remember him. He'd loved music, and we knew some very good singers in our village. We decided that on the anniversary of his death, rather than mope at home, we would put on a musical evening to celebrate his life and his love of music, and to raise money for our chosen charities: Children in Need (our favourite charity ever since Mac had moved in on Children in Need night 2008) and the road safety charity Brake (as they had supported us with bereavement advice since Mac had died).

We spent the rest of the year planning and rehearsing. It felt like such a good thing to be doing, and it certainly gave me something positive to focus on. We also organised a raffle and an auction of two original paintings by very good local artists who produced the artwork specifically for the occasion. We pulled together songs that Mac loved, and others that we knew would be fun and mean that we could have an enjoyable evening celebrating all that Mac was. I compèred the evening and reprised my 'Song of the King' from the musical *Joseph and the Amazing Technicolor Dreamcoat* from some years before. (My representation of Elvis was definitely from his later years, when the fried banana and peanut butter sandwiches had started to take their toll!)

The running order was:

First Half
1. 'Seasons of Love' from Rent, *performed by the chorus.*
2. Various, performed by Ines and Charlie S.
3. 'Nothing' from A Chorus Line, *performed by Rebecca.*

4. 'A Spoonful of Sugar' from Mary Poppins, *performed by Charlie C.*

5. 'Popular' from Wicked, *performed by Sally.*

6. 'Defying Gravity' from Wicked, *performed by Olivia.*

7. 'For Good' from Wicked, *performed by Rebecca and Olivia.*

8. The Sound of Music *medley, performed by the chorus.*

Second Half

1. 'Song of the King' from Joseph and the Amazing Technicolor Dreamcoat, *performed by Richard.*

2. 'Do You Hear the People Sing?' from Les Misérables, *performed by the chorus.*

3. 'With You' from Ghost, *performed by Sally.*

4. 'Big Spender' from Sweet Charity, *performed by Jonathan and Craig.*

5. 'Tell Me It's Not True' from Blood Brothers, *performed by Rebecca and the chorus.*

6. 'Any Dream Will Do' from Joseph and the Amazing Technicolor Dreamcoat, *performed by the chorus.*

7. 'Sparkle and Shine' from Nativity!, *performed by the chorus.*

8. 'Seasons of Love' from Rent, *performed by the chorus.*

We opened and closed with 'Seasons of Love' from *Rent*. It had been a favourite of mine and Swee's for many years and Mac had also grown to love it. The lyrics talk about measuring a year in love – the perfect sentiment to mark a year since Mac had died.

We were lucky that the composer of the song 'Sparkle and Shine' from the film *Nativity!* allowed us to use the music. Mac's godmother had managed to track her down to get the music and gain permission. Mac adored the film, and we used to laugh and laugh at the antics of Mr Poppy and the children. 'Sparkle and Shine' was a special moment for all of us.

The evening was a success. It was an occasion for so many of the people who had been close to Mac to come together and celebrate. I had been nervous about how I would feel, standing up, talking about Mac, and hearing and singing all of those wonderful songs – I didn't want to break down in front of everyone. I shouldn't have worried. Of course, there were a few lumps in the throat – we had chosen some songs that were bound to have that effect – but the evening as a whole was positive and uplifting. It also raised £5,000 for our charities. We couldn't have been happier.

And with that, the first year was over.

Chapter 22

Being Mac's Mum: Thoughts from Swee

Special occasions

Being a mum is a big job. When a fully formed eight-year-old arrives in your home to stay for good, he'll tell you what you need to know to do your job.

In the run-up to his birthday, Mac said, "Mum, because you haven't been a mum before, these are the things you need to know about birthdays…"

- You need to put balloons on the door.
- You have to buy birthday tablecloths, serviettes and paper plates.
- You need a birthday cake with candles.
- You need goody bags and banners.
- You need to invite my friends to come.
- We need sausages, pizza, sandwiches, jelly and ice cream.

Of course, all of these requests were fulfilled. For the first time in his life, Mac was like other eight-year-olds. That went down well.

He was exhausted, and tumbled into bed to have happy birthday dreams.

Every birthday after that was of concern to him: would it be as good as the last one? Luckily, it always was. One year Richard made the tallest rainbow cake. I iced it and covered it in Haribo sweets. It looked amazing! It was August and extremely hot – the cake seemed like the Leaning Tower of Pisa. Holding it in the car on the way to the party venue, I screamed all the way. Pisa wasn't built in a day. (I know it's Rome!)

Mac wasn't well in the run-up to his first Christmas with us. Dr Pat said he could alternate Calpol and ibuprofen every few hours. He eventually sweated out a fever and we learned that it was the sachets of strawberry Calpol that helped him the most. (He spat out the orange-flavour ibuprofen!) He remembered this feeling of vulnerability at later dates. He always found comfort in our super king-sized bed, and often started his night there.

We must have visited Asda, M&S and Next many a time. He loved to buy presents for people. His dad's birthday was cause for much preparation, purchasing and presents. Woe betide me if I bought cufflinks more than once (which I did!). I was told off! There were special hiding places for presents, and Mac never gave away any secrets. He gleaned lots of happiness from his efforts and brought much joy to those on the receiving end.

Junior school

When I drove Mac to school in the morning he would always ask what was happening after school. Most evenings we went with his friends Bailey and Connor to the recreation ground and ran off some steam. In the summer we would end up at Bailey's home, where his mum fixed up a ground slide and a huge paddling pool. The boys frolicked and shrieked with excitement, racing and jumping into the pool. They were all great mates, accepting each other for who they were.

Bailey came for his first sleepover and ate lots of sweets and drank lots of pop, camping out in our converted garage and enjoying a full English breakfast the following morning. I clearly remember the two of them in sleeping bags, sliding down the stairs, timing each other to race for the prize of being number one.

In the winter we did a lot of cooking. Mac set up his own cake-baking business and we made hundreds of chocolate cupcakes, iced shortbread stars, and delicious loaf cakes with marshmallow and chocolate topping. He later went on to make these on his own. His skill at producing the most amazing shortbread was legendary.

Mac loved creating art with me. We painted a portrait of Richard, and a waterfall – two canvases we still hold dear. Mac was so proud of them. We collaged a piece called *Fish and Chips*, which was also a great success.

Playground politics and snotty mums

I was one of the outsiders – three mums who waited for our kids at the edge of the playground under the big oak tree. The green welly brigade performed centre stage, drove their four-by-fours very badly, often wore pristine white jeans, but never had a kind word for anyone. In fact their blame culture was astounding. If they didn't know the details of the situation they concocted a range of foul untruths. The teachers were always on our side, and not once in all his time at primary school was Mac at fault for the things others blamed on him. In fact, it was quite the opposite. He wrongly took the blame for writing on the classroom wall because he didn't want the class to be punished, but a very intuitive teacher realised that the culprit was another little boy.

Some other children made up tales of Mac's misdoings – but they were just tales. One mum rang me on behalf of another (!) to accuse Mac of using words he didn't use. They sounded like those of an older brother who knew the F-word and combined it with the name of one of the girls in their class – wrong, wrong, wrong! Mac was not at all sexualised, and was actually quite innocent for his age – the insinuation was a sad reflection of privileged children who are spoiled and spiteful and mums who don't know how to behave. Until that incident, I didn't have a voice, but that tiger mum instinct kicked in and I don't think anyone will forget what I said. Ultimately, I believe in karma.

These mums came to Mac's memorial – deduce what you will from that. I can forgive, but I don't forget.

Secondary school

Mac's first secondary school didn't quite get him. Information was not passed on and I spent endless hours in reception, meeting specialists who were able to make suggestions for the better. However, as I said, the information was never passed on to the relevant people. Consequently, a male computer studies teacher raised his voice to Mac, which rarely worked, especially if he had not been in the wrong. Mac refused to move and stopped the classes from moving around. A very frustrated teacher called me in.

On seeing Mac I knew he was OK, but angry. I said, "You look unhappy, sweetie."

"I am!" was the response.

So, I encouraged him to go to the car and eat what treats I'd left him in the glovebox. He was fine as we drove home. I am ashamed to say that we laughed about this many times. He wasn't a bad lad. We ate scrambled egg on toast with bacon, and his equilibrium was restored.

Dressing up

Dressing up was a joy to Mac. He was asked to be an ancient Greek for school. We managed the white sheet and dressing-gown cord as his toga, together with his sandals. He looked great. What we didn't agree on was the crown of laurels. At 1am, I stepped out onto a cold patio and picked leaves from the bay tree to make a wreath/crown for his head. After breakfast he was off to school, laurel crown in his hand, refusing to wear it.

On picking him up from school that afternoon, I found he had won a prize for his 'authentic crown'. He was thrilled; brownie points for Mum, and he learned to trust me a bit more.

Valentine

Valentine's Day, and another trip to Asda. Mac (then aged eleven) had made friends with Lilly (aged twelve) from the village, who'd befriended him at the school bus stop. He asked if he could buy her gifts and a card. I spoke to Lilly's mum to get permission for him to deliver them. She was a little shocked but said it was OK.

I drove Mac up to their house and he gave Lilly her presents, saying, "Thank you for being a good friend."

Delightful, sweet, not forgotten. Lilly wrote a card at his memorial with love from his Valentine.

Church

On Mothering Sunday, and whenever I was in church, Mac would come down at the peace to give me a kiss. It was all about his ownership of and pride in me. He was growing stronger in mind and body. I recall on our first Mother's Day he was the last one to leave the altar. He spent ages choosing a blue soap wrapped in a blue flannel, because blue is my favourite colour. I love him for that.

He had to be involved in the joint funeral of my parents, who had died eight days apart. He read at the memorial and then, on returning to our pew, burst into tears. He shook with pain, and leaned into me for solace. He loved them dearly, and at their care home he would often go off to meet with Grandma on his own. He was able to empathise with her frailty and vulnerability.

He also came to Winchester Cathedral for our vicar Michael's funeral. He sang and grieved. He really did miss him. The service was wonderful – that day we saw a glimpse of heaven. I hope Mac met all of them there.

Honouring Mac is easy. We miss him every day. Our life will never be the same since he went away.

Chapter 23

Life After Mac

As I write this chapter, eight years have now passed since Mac died. It's a significant milestone in many ways. First, because eight years is a long time. But it is particularly significant in Mac's life (and death) because he lived eight years before he moved in with us, he lived with us for eight years, and he has now been dead for eight years.

So, this seems like a good point to reflect on some things I've thought about since Mac died.

Grief

Grief is a strange animal. I've read loads of descriptions of and poems about grief since Mac died – and in their way, they all describe some of what you find yourself living with.

For me, the one that resonates most is the image of grief as a person walking beside you. At first the grief is holding on to you, reaching into your heart, constantly there and pulling away at your insides. Then slowly, bit by bit, grief starts to loosen his grip on you. You start to walk a little easier; the hurt is no longer ever-present. But occasionally, he gets in your way and makes you stumble; he grabs at you and the pain comes back. These times begin to become less frequent, less intense, until eventually you reach a steady state: grief is walking behind you. He doesn't impede your progress any more, but you know he's there. Sometimes he might tap you on the shoulder, just to remind you – but the hurt is less and the memories are good.

I think that is where I am now. And from time to time, the tap comes. You can't always predict what it might be. For me, music is one of my key triggers. A few years ago, an album of covers was released to raise money for Children in Need. The songs were all covered by famous actors. The whole album is fantastic, and for a cause close to our hearts – but two songs particularly resonated with me: 'Yellow' by Jodie Whittaker and 'Never Grow Up' by Shaun Dooley. 'Yellow' was poignant because Jodie dedicated it to her nephew who had died recently. And 'Never Grow Up' has words that I think all parents can relate to as they see their children growing up so fast before their eyes.

Mac and I used to listen to music together all the time in the car. He would gently tease me for my taste, and then later he would choose to play a song that he knew I liked, and he secretly liked as well. I find myself missing those times – but what I really miss are the conversations that we might have today. I listen to my friends talking about the conversations and relationships they have with their grown-up children, and while I revel in them and love to hear them, doing so will always be accompanied by a pang as that is something I can never have. There will be no new conversations with Mac: the conversations I have with him in my head will go unanswered.

Being a dad was such a huge part of my identity. It was hard-won, something that I loved so much (even the really hard bits), and something I think I was good at. I felt protective of Mac as soon as he walked through our door and we became a family.

I used to love to join in with conversations with my friends and colleagues about their children: comparing notes, sharing tips, laughing at the latest teenage mishaps. And of course, I can still do that now – but I worry that the stories I share start to feel a bit lame; somewhat past their sell-by date. And if it's someone who doesn't know, how do you answer the question, "And how old are your children?" I can tell you, there's no better way to destroy an atmosphere than to tell someone your child has died! But I still want to join in, and I do.

When Mac first died, I remember asking myself, "Am I still a dad?" Everyone told me not to be stupid – of course I was. But I realised that there is no name for what I had become: if you lose your parents you are an orphan; if you lose your partner you are a widow or widower. There is no word for a bereaved parent.

As I said earlier, grief walks behind you and sometimes taps you on the shoulder. And whenever I hear about someone dying before their time, the tap comes on my shoulder. It makes me think of the things that Mac has missed. It makes me realise that this year he would be twenty-four, and that is very hard to imagine. Whenever I hear of a parent whose child has died, it makes me think about all of the people who are affected, the ripples in the pond of life – just like all the ripples we felt when we realised how many people had been affected by Mac's death. But mostly, I remember that there is another set of parents out there who have lost a child way before their time, and who will begin on the journey they never thought they would have to take – and I pray for them.

The missing part of Mac's story

For a long time after Mac died, I did not dwell on the circumstances of his death – I didn't want to think about them. Even now, when it is reported that someone has died in a motorcycle accident, it doesn't immediately connect with me that that is the way that Mac died. The reality for me is that one day he left to go to school, and the next time I saw him he was lying peacefully in a hospital morgue. I couldn't deal with the violence of his death.

But more than that, I think, is that underlying it all, there was a guilt that I couldn't keep him safe, and that I wasn't with him when he died. I have always felt that even though I couldn't protect him from that final threat, I should at least have been with him as he passed. As part of a project, an artist friend of mine asked people to write down what they were sorry for, and it was clear for me that my contribution had to be 'I'm sorry I wasn't there when you died.'

As time moved on, and as I thought more about this, I decided I wanted to see if I could find out who *was* with him when he died, and more about what had happened. I contacted the police, and in a remarkably short time they found the names and contact details of the witnesses. With some trepidation, I wrote emails of thanks and hoped to hear from them.

And a wonderful woman called Emma wrote back. She had been first on the scene of the crash. When she got there Mac was standing up – the adrenaline keeping him on his feet. She helped to get him to the roadside, and to lay him down and make him comfortable. She looked for his licence so that she could call him by his name, and she just spoke to him and stroked him and comforted him and made sure he was never alone. She and some others who joined her made sure that he was warm, and stayed with him until the emergency services took him away. She was able to tell me how hard everyone had worked and how gentle they were with him, carefully removing his helmet and stroking his arm and his face to make sure he knew he wasn't alone and that he was loved.

It is hard to put into words the gratitude I have for the people who were with Mac, but particularly for Emma. And what she probably doesn't realise is that she has laid to rest the two main fears that Swee and I had: I was always worried that no one was comforting him and caring for him, and Swee was always worried that he was cold. In that reply, Emma was able to answer those questions for us.

So that part of Mac's story is now put to rest. Emma was the angel Mac needed at that time, and I am so very glad that she was there to help him. Emma – thank you.

Do memories fade?

I have always fancied myself as having a very good memory. Certainly, when I was younger, I never forgot anything. I was always able to remember trivial facts, and I seldom had to revise hard for my exams. I did a lot of acting at home and at university, and learning long scripts was never a chore, or something to which I gave a second thought.

Now, anyone reading this who has worked with me or who knows me really well is probably laughing quietly to themselves. It is true that, now that I am in my sixth decade, my memory isn't what it was. I find that I need to make lists and be reminded of things that I am meant to do. But on the whole, I think my memory is still pretty good.

Then, the other day, I was sitting in the sitting room and looking at the pictures on our wall. One of them is a collage made up of a number of pictures of Mac, Swee and me. As a gift, when Mac came to live with us, some good friends bought us a professional photography session. It was the perfect gift. Taken so early in our time together as a family, those photos show something of the fun and hope that we had as a newly formed unit: us against the world. We had hundreds of photos taken – so much so, it took a very long time to choose the best ones – but we now have some fantastic images as a clear memory of that time. There are ones of the three of us, but also some wonderful ones of Mac dressed as a wizard, and holding one of his most prized possessions at the time: a ceramic motorbike that he had painted himself.

But as I looked at the pictures, it felt as though all of that had happened to someone else. Yes, I could remember the occasion; I could remember how much fun we had, and how carefully Swee had picked out clothes for us that would look good in the photos. But somehow it all seemed so distant. It felt as though I was losing that memory; as if it was another lifetime. I went to find Swee, and for the first time in a long time, I sobbed and sobbed. It made me so sad to think that maybe my memories of Mac and of being a dad were fading away.

But then I thought more about the nature of memories. It is true that parts of our memories fade. One of the main reasons I wanted to write down my memories of bringing up Mac and our time together is that one day I will find it harder to remember, and

I don't want his life, and the memories of all that he was, to die with me. I want there to be something more lasting to honour him.

So, is it inevitable that my memories will fade? I guess in some ways it is. One of my greatest fears has been that one day our eight years together will seem like such a short part of my life – it's already eight years since Mac died. But I do know that those years were the most important time in my life – it doesn't mean that what went before, or what will come after, is not equally important. Being a husband, a son, a brother, an uncle, a godfather, a boss, a friend, a priest – all of these things define me. All of them have changed me and made me who I am. Just as being a dad to Mac has been one of the most important things – made all the more precious by being taken away all too soon.

What I do know about memories is that certain things come back very easily, and don't seem to fade at all. My gran died in 1997 – I loved her dearly, and I can still feel her hug, made strong by years of manual housework. I can still feel her unconditional love. I can still hear her soft Wearside accent. And with Mac, I don't think I will ever forget the feeling of complete love that I had for him; I won't forget singing with him in the car; I won't forget the way he bumped clumsily up the stairs like a deer that hadn't grown into his long limbs; and I won't forget his laugh. But most of all it is the feelings that can come back in an instant. So maybe the memories will fade, but I know the feelings never will.

Chapter 24

Final Thoughts

I had always considered writing about our experience of bringing up Mac. When we were looking to adopt, there was not much that you could read that gave a realistic sense of what bringing up an older adopted child was like. I thought that some of our experiences might be useful for others. Then there were the funny memories – the stories we tell around the dinner table or when new girlfriends are introduced (the verbal equivalent of the naked baby picture) – that seemed like they would be fun to record somewhere. Again, it was just for us as a family, but if others were interested and found our reminiscences useful, then it felt a good thing to do.

And then Mac died. Of course, that turned our life and our plans on their head. It is impossible to say here just how much it changed Swee and me as people and changed the way we think about so much.

But as I thought about it more, it struck me that the people with whom you share the majority of your memories are usually your children. Your memories are part of the inheritance that you pass on; part of the way that you live on in them, shaping them with your love, your care, and your stories about the past. Of course,

Swee and I are no longer in a position to do that – so here I offer our memories to you. Writing this was a way to get those memories on paper; to share them with people. I think our story is a good one and worth sharing, at the very least with our friends and family. It was also a way to ensure that Swee and I had a record of as many of our memories as we could.

But this became even more important on 18 September 2020, the day before Swee's sixtieth birthday – the day that Swee died.

She had become more and more sedentary and housebound after Mac died, and she had suffered from a number of unrelated illnesses. I am sure that the loss of Mac really took away most of the purpose in her life. That isn't to say that she wasn't happy – she was. But there was no reason to get up and get better, and in the end, her body gave up. This was about six months into the Covid lockdown, and lockdown had been a positive experience for us in many ways because Swee and I got to spend her last six months together without me having to commute up to London every day.

I am very lucky that I have a wonderful family around me, but with Swee gone, these memories became even more important to me as I was the sole custodian of them all. I wanted them written down somewhere and shared more widely to let them live on.

I wasn't sure where to end this book. I have always wanted for it to be a positive thing – something that celebrates Mac's life and the man that he was becoming, and how we got there. I wanted it to be a book that celebrated how we found Mac and helped him to find himself; how we helped him to mature, build resilience and learn to live with the things that had happened to him in the past; and how he learned to keep his old life and his new life in balance. I wanted it to tell of the wonderful memories I have, and how lucky we were to have him in our lives. I didn't want it to concentrate on how he died, but it would be wrong to ignore his death and how it affected us because we learned so much about who we were and are as parents by losing him – leaving that out just didn't seem right.

I haven't mentioned anywhere the court case against the man who was driving the van that killed Mac. It is a matter of public record, so if anyone is interested it is possible to find the details. Enough to say that eventually, after some months of pleading not guilty, the accused pleaded guilty to the charge of causing death by careless driving and received a prison sentence of twenty months (of which he served about five). He also received a two-year ban and will be required to retake his driving test before he regains his licence.

Many of our friends commented on how short the sentence was – but I was never looking for retribution. I'm not sure that being locked up for a number of months was any worse for him than knowing that he had killed a sixteen-year-old in his prime. What I do struggle with is the fact that in all likelihood he will drive again. It turned out that he had a number of driving convictions and had been banned in the past. The judge made the comment that he considered the van driver a very bad driver, and that Mac's driving had been exemplary. But Mac is dead and that man will drive again.

But back to the positive: what lessons did we take from becoming Mac's parents that we might pass on to other adoptive parents (and some of them are just as applicable to any parent!)?

- You will need support from family and friends. You might be surprised by how some people react.
- Remember that your child's story is for them to share, and to choose whom to share it with.

- Even if you find you have had enough of social services during the approval process, build a good relationship as they can be useful if you need access to advice or support as your child grows up.
- Work hand in hand with schools and other professionals.
- Meet other adoptive parents; they will understand some of the unique issues that come with adoption. As one once said to me, our children are different.
- Expect to have to deal with issues to do with your child's past several times as they mature and begin to understand them on different levels.
- Don't be afraid of contact with the birth family. It is better for you to be involved, and contact is inevitable with the advances in social media.
- Be open and honest about the birth family, but never judgemental (however much you want to be!).
- Decide what you need to control, and where you can hand control over to your child – they are desperate to get some control back in their life.
- Learn from your mistakes. Use your instincts, but also be prepared to parent 'intellectually'.
- Don't label your child unless it is helpful and necessary. They already have one big label that makes them different: adopted.
- Don't look for problems. Look for the gaps and help your child to fill them.
- Make memories. None of us knows how long we have.
- Above all, love your child. Love them unconditionally. And have fun – they are children for a very short time.

Time moves on. The pain of losing a child never goes away – but you do learn to live with it, and in time it doesn't become what defines you (unless you allow it to). The pain is inevitable – it is the absence of love. There are occasions when things are worse: celebrating my fiftieth birthday was not the same without my son by my side in the way he was when we celebrated Swee's. As his peers move on and grow up, it reminds me of the future that has been lost for all of us. Sometimes these occasions catch me unawares, and the tears just come from nowhere.

We learned to prepare and to create new traditions. We weren't sure what to do on Mac's eighteenth birthday. So we gathered together – family and our closest friends – and had a birthday party. We had a rainbow cake and released balloons – and it might be fanciful, but as the balloons rose up into the sky, they formed an 'M'.

Of course I miss him. I miss his laugh that sounded like a peal of bells. I miss his bear hugs. I miss singing with him in the car. But if someone had told me that we would only have him for eight years and that we would have to endure the pain of losing our son, I would still do it without a moment's hesitation.

And now that Swee has gone as well, I wanted even more to share this story and these memories with all of you. Losing a partner is very different to losing a child. Half of us in long-term relationships will experience the loss of a partner, but thankfully few of us experience the loss of a child. But this is never a matter of competitive grieving. In some ways, Swee's death was harder than Mac's – but that is because it was for me the cumulative effect of losing all of my perfect little nuclear family, and when Mac died I'd had Swee to help me through it.

When Mac died, someone told me that I would never be the same again, and I remember thinking that that was a really dreadful thing to say. But of course, it is true. For at least a couple of years after Swee died I was in a pretty dark place: rarely going out, and questioning what the rest of my life was all about. Now, in 2024, I can finally say that I am happy again. I have been lucky enough to finish full-time work early and to have the time to do all sorts of hobbies, spend more time in church, enjoy the wonderful village I live in, and spend time with family and friends. I was lucky to have that one true love in Swee – my soulmate – and that is always something worth celebrating as we don't all get that opportunity.

I think it is true that I might never be as happy again as I was being a dad and a husband, and of course I wish that Swee and Mac were still here with me. But that does not mean I'm not happy – I am, and I know that I am very lucky in all that I have. But the main subject of this book was always Mac: the journey to finding him, and how he found himself as he grew up.

My last thoughts: being a parent, however that is achieved, is a privilege and the best job in the world. It can be so easy to take it for granted if we are not careful. The truth is that we learn so much more from our children than they can ever learn from us, and I know that I am an infinitely better person for having been Mac's dad.

Sparkle and shine, my beautiful boy. I love you.
Dad xxx

Macaully Richard George Sutcliffe
17 August 2000 – 14 October 2016